LAW COMMISSION

CRIMINAL LAW: CONSPIRACY TO DEFRAUD

CONTENTS

The Law Commission

(LAW COM.No.228)

CRIMINAL LAW: CONSPIRACY TO DEFRAUD

Item 5 of the Fourth Programme of Law Reform: Criminal Law

Laid before Parliament by the Lord High Chancellor pursuant to section 3(2) of the Law Commissions Act 1965

Ordered by The House of Commons *to be printed*
6 December 1994

LONDON: HMSO
£10.85 net

The Law Commission was set up by section 1 of the Law Commissions Act 1965 for the purpose of promoting the reform of the law.

The Commissioners are:

> The Honourable Mr Justice Brooke, *Chairman*
> Professor Andrew Burrows
> Miss Diana Faber
> Mr Charles Harpum
> Mr Stephen Silber QC

The Secretary of the Law Commission is Mr Michael Sayers and its offices are at Conquest House, 37-38 John Street, Theobalds Road, London, WC1N 2BQ.

LAW COMMISSION

Item 5 of the Fourth Programme of Law Reform: Criminal Law

CRIMINAL LAW: CONSPIRACY TO DEFRAUD

To the Right Honourable the Lord Mackay of Clashfern, Lord High Chancellor of Great Britain

PART I
INTRODUCTION

1.1 In this report we consider conspiracy to defraud, which remains a common law offence. Although there is no general offence of fraud as such in English law, conspiracy to defraud comes close to being such an offence, since its scope is extremely wide.[1] However, as its name indicates, it cannot be committed by one person acting alone.

A.   BACKGROUND TO THE REPORT

1.   Our work on conspiracy generally

1.2 In our Second Programme of Law Reform[2] we recommended a comprehensive examination of the criminal law with a view to its codification. In 1970 work began on the law of conspiracy, the task being committed to a Working Party comprising two Commissioners and representatives of the Criminal Law Revision Committee and the Home Office. The Working Party examined conspiracy in the context of inchoate offences generally, and at an early stage in its work it provisionally decided that the offence of conspiracy should be restricted, as under the existing law it was not, to conspiracy to commit a substantive offence. That approach implied that, since a conspiracy to do anything other than commit a substantive offence would no longer found liability, conspiracy should be considered in conjunction with work on the inchoate offences (such as attempts), which necessarily involved the contemplated commission of a substantive offence.

1.3 In 1973 the Working Party published a consultation document,[3] in which it examined conspiracy in the context of inchoate offences. In that paper the Working Party considered at length the question whether conspiracy should be confined to agreement to commit an offence. It concluded emphatically that there should be no place in a criminal code for a law of conspiracy extending beyond that ambit.

---

[1]   See Part II below.

[2]   (1968) Law Com No 14, Item XVIII. See now our Fourth Programme of Law Reform (1989) Law Com No 185, Cm 800, Item 5.

[3]   Working Paper No 50, Inchoate Offences.

1.4 The Working Party recommended, however, that before this major proposal was implemented, the Commission should examine the relevant areas of the law with a view to identifying and, where necessary, filling gaps which would be left by a limitation of conspiracy in the way proposed. In accordance with this approach, the Commission published in 1974 and 1975 a series of working papers, including one, Working Paper No 56 ("WP 56"), on conspiracy to defraud.

1.5 In 1976 we published our report on conspiracy,[4] in which we recommended that in general conspiracy should be limited to agreements to commit a substantive offence. This recommendation was implemented by Part I of the Criminal Law Act 1977 (hereafter "the 1977 Act"). Section 1 of the Act enacted a statutory offence of conspiracy, to replace the common law offence of conspiracy. The provision embodied the general principle, widely supported on consultation, that conduct should not be criminal merely because two or more persons agree to perform it. Conspiracy was to be an offence only if the object of the conspiracy would necessarily amount to the commission of a crime.

1.6 Exceptionally, however, we excluded conspiracy to defraud from the ambit of this recommendation. We expressed the view[5] that the use of conspiracy charges in the field of fraud, though sometimes undesirable, did not merit criticism to the same extent as could properly be levelled at their use in other areas. We went on to say that in WP 56[6] a number of lacunae had been identified which our proposed general restriction of conspiracy would leave in the field of fraud; that the Commission's eventual aim was to produce a draft "fraud" Bill which would take its place in a Code beside the Theft Act 1968; that such a task would be difficult and raise problems "both of policy and technique"; and that a report on conspiracy to defraud would therefore take a considerable time to produce. No firm proposals had at the time been put forward for anything to be put in the place of conspiracy to defraud.[7] To have abolished that offence without any statutory replacement would have left an unacceptable gap in the law. Abolition would be possible only when suitable offences had been devised.

1.7 In consequence, conspiracy to defraud was excluded from the 1977 Act. Section 5(2) provided:

> Subsection (1) above [abolishing the offence of conspiracy at common law] shall not affect the offence of conspiracy at common law so far as relates to conspiracy to defraud, *and section 1 above shall not apply in any*

---

[4] Criminal Law: Conspiracy and Criminal Law Reform (1976) Law Com No 76, HC 176.

[5] *Ibid,* paras 1.14-1.16.

[6] See para 1.4 above.

[7] Law Com No 76, para 1.16.

case where the agreement in question amounts to a conspiracy to defraud at common law.[8]

2. Restrictions on charging conspiracy to defraud following the Criminal Law Act 1977

1.8 The words in section 5(2) of the 1977 Act that we have emphasised in the preceding paragraph gave rise to a conflict of judicial opinion as to whether conspiracy to defraud could be properly charged where the facts also revealed a statutory conspiracy, under section 1 of the Act, to commit a substantive offence. The conflict was resolved by the House of Lords in *Ayres*,[9] which held that conspiracy to defraud could not be charged in such circumstances. Lord Bridge, whose reasoning was adopted by the other law lords, expressed the view that the ruling would not create undue difficulty for prosecutors or judges:

> In the overwhelming majority of conspiracy cases it will be obvious that performance of the agreement which constitutes the conspiracy would necessarily involve, and frequently will in fact have already involved, the commission of one or more substantive offences by one or more of the conspirators. In such cases one or more counts of conspiracy, as appropriate, should be charged under section 1 of the Act. Only the exceptional fraudulent agreements will need to be charged as common law conspiracies to defraud, when either it is clear that performance of the agreement constituting the conspiracy would not have involved the commission by any conspirator of any substantive offence or it is uncertain whether or not it would do so. In case of doubt, it may be appropriate to include two counts in the indictment in the alternative. It would then be for the judge to decide how to leave the case to the jury at the conclusion of the evidence, bearing always in mind that the crucial issue is whether performance of the agreement constituting the conspiracy would necessarily involve the commission of a substantive offence by a conspirator. If it would, it is a section 1 conspiracy. If it would not, it is a common law conspiracy to defraud.[10]

1.9 Subsequent experience of prosecutions involving large-scale frauds revealed, however, that this restriction on the use of charges of conspiracy to defraud gave rise to considerable difficulties and to injustice in some cases. The effect of *Ayres* was mitigated in *Cooke*,[11] in which Lord Bridge recognised[12] the need to "modify the

---

[8] Emphasis added.

[9] [1984] AC 447.

[10] [1984] AC 447, 459H-460C.

[11] [1986] AC 909.

[12] [1986] AC 909, 918.

language" he had used in *Ayres* to avoid some of the difficulties that that decision had caused. The House of Lords, while confirming the ruling in *Ayres* that statutory conspiracy and conspiracy to defraud were mutually exclusive, held that, where it could be shown that there had been an agreed course of conduct going beyond an agreement to commit specific offences, it was legitimate to charge either conspiracy to defraud on its own or both conspiracy to defraud and a statutory conspiracy to commit the specific offences. Even after *Cooke*, however, where the execution of the alleged conspiracy to defraud would involve the commission of substantive offences, the prosecutor had to show that he could prove some essential ingredient in the fraud which was not an element in any of the substantive offences.[13]

3. The Roskill Report

1.10 The Roskill Committee[14] (which reported before the decision in *Cooke*) referred to the concern among prosecutors that *Ayres* had engendered, and continued:

> In many fraud cases a charge of a substantive offence or of a statutory conspiracy to commit a substantive offence will be entirely appropriate and the maximum penalties adequate. In some cases, however, the only substantive offence available may be a relatively minor offence carrying a low penalty or a series of minor offences, or an offence or offences which are perhaps only incidental to the fraud. In these circumstances, the prosecution may find it impossible to prosecute for offences which reflect the totality and gravity of the allegedly fraudulent conduct in what would otherwise be called conspiracy to defraud. As one submission to us put it, there is a risk of "a build up [of] a case history of thwarted or inappropriate prosecutions for major frauds".[15]

4. The statutory reversal of *Ayres*

1.11 In 1986, very shortly after the Roskill Committee reported, the Home Secretary of the day asked the Criminal Law Revision Committee (the "CLRC") to review, as a matter of urgency, the restrictions on the use of a charge of conspiracy to defraud in the light of the decision in *Ayres* (and subsequent cases).[16] Later that year the

---

[13] Professor J C Smith, [1986] Crim LR 236.

[14] Report of the Fraud Trials Committee (1986). The Committee's terms of reference, set out in para 1.1 of the Report, were:

> to consider in what ways the conduct of criminal proceedings in England and Wales arising from fraud can be improved and to consider what changes in existing law and procedure would be desirable to secure the just, expeditious and economical disposal of such proceedings.

[15] *Ibid*, para 3.11.

[16] *Cooke* (para 1.9 above), however, was decided too late for consideration by the CLRC.

CLRC published its Report on the matter.[17] In one Part of its Report,[18] which we set out in Appendix B hereto, the CLRC examined several decisions since *Ayres* which involved difficulties that had arisen out of the construction placed by the House of Lords in that case on section 5(2) of the Criminal Law Act 1977.[19] The CLRC's main recommendation, that *Ayres* should be reversed by legislation,[20] was implemented by section 12(1) of the Criminal Justice Act 1987.[21] Section 12(1) does not apply to "things done" before 20 July 1987, the date on which it came into force;[22] so that *Ayres* (as qualified by *Cooke*) restricts the availability of conspiracy to defraud where the conspiracy was made before that date, unless it continued in being thereafter.[23]

5. Law Commission Working Paper No 104

1.12 Later in 1987 we published a consultative document, Working Paper No 104 (hereafter "WP 104"), which superseded WP 56,[24] and in which we comprehensively reviewed conspiracy to defraud and invited comments on a range of possible options for reform.

---

[17] Criminal Law Revision Committee, Eighteenth Report, Conspiracy to Defraud (1986) Cmnd 9873.

[18] *Ibid*, Part III.

[19] The text of this subsection is set out in para 1.7 above.

[20] The CLRC further recommended that the guidelines contained in the Code for Crown Prosecutors which is published under section 10 of the Prosecution of Offences Act 1985 should include guidance on the circumstances in which it was appropriate to charge conspiracy to defraud. Such guidelines have now been issued: see para 2.16 below.

[21] Section 12 (1) provides:

If -

(a) a person agrees with any other person or persons that a course of conduct shall be pursued; and

(b) that course of conduct will necessarily amount to or involve the commission of any offence or offences by one or more of the parties to the agreement if the agreement is carried out in accordance with their intentions,

the fact that it will do so shall not preclude a charge of conspiracy to defraud being brought against any of them in respect of the agreement.

Consequentially, s 12(2) of the 1987 Act repealed the concluding words of section 5(2) of the Criminal Law Act 1977 (see para 1.7 above).

[22] SI 1987 No 1061.

[23] *Boyle and Mears* (1992) 94 Cr App R 158.

[24] See para 1.4 above. Our reasons for producing a further consultative document were that: (1) further work on the proposals in WP 56 had been held up by "the need to complete work on other projects and for other reasons"; (2) there had been a number of substantial changes in the law since the publication of WP 56; and (3) insufficient weight had been given in WP 56 to the procedural and other advantages of charging conspiracy to defraud: WP 104, para 1.7.

6. Developments in the law after publication of Working Paper No 104

1.13 Significant judicial development of the scope of conspiracy to defraud has taken place since WP 104 was published,[25] and legislation has been enacted in relation to the misuse of computers.[26] Legislation has also been put in place which, when brought into force, will considerably extend the territorial jurisdiction of the English courts to try a number of substantive and inchoate offences of fraud and dishonesty, including both conspiracy to commit a substantive offence and conspiracy to defraud.[27]

7. Our subsequent work on the project

1.14 The consultation period on WP 104 ended on 30 June 1988 and the responses were subsequently analysed. It was hoped to prepare the final report in 1989,[28] but work on this project did not proceed as rapidly as we would have wished, owing to the need to devote an increased level of resources to the Computer Misuse project.[29] Work continued on the project but further intensive studies demonstrated the complex nature of the difficulties involved, and progress was delayed because staff were required for other projects in 1990.[30] The need to devote resources to other more pressing criminal law reform projects continued and in addition it became necessary to analyse the practical implications of the project in the light of more recent developments. Our criminal law team conducted detailed consultations with various prosecution authorities and, under the aegis of the Confederation of British Industry, with a number of commercial and industrial organisations.[31] In addition the impending departure of Richard Buxton QC[32] from the Commission on 31 December 1993 resulted in some re-ordering of priorities within the team in 1993, with the result that work on this project was again delayed.[33]

1.15 During 1993 we conducted consultations with interested parties with a view to eliciting the uses to which, by that date, conspiracy to defraud had come to be put,

---

[25] See, in particular, *Moses* (para 2.7 below) and *Wai Yu-tsang* (para 2.8 below).

[26] Computer Misuse Act 1990. The Act is based on the recommendations in our Report on Computer Misuse (1989) Law Com No 186, Cm 819.

[27] Criminal Justice Act 1993, Part I; see paras 2.21-2.22 below. This part of the Act is based on the recommendations in our report Criminal Law: Jurisdiction over Offences of Fraud and Dishonesty with a Foreign Element (1989) Law Com No 180, HC 318.

[28] Twenty-Third Annual Report 1987-1988 (1989) Law Com No 176, HC 227, para 2.9.

[29] Twenty-Fourth Annual Report 1989 (1990) Law Com No 190, HC 215, para 2.14. See our report Criminal Law: Computer Misuse (1989) Law Com No 186, Cm 819.

[30] Twenty-fifth Annual Report 1990 (1991) Law Com No 195, HC 249, para 2.19.

[31] Twenty-Sixth Annual Report 1991 (1992) Law Com No 206, HC 280, para 2.24; Twenty-Seventh Annual Report 1992 (1993) Law Com No 210, HC 518, paras 2.25, 2.45 and 2.47.

[32] Now the Hon Mr Justice Buxton.

[33] Twenty-Eighth Annual Report 1993 (1994) Law Com No 223, HC 341, para 2.47.

and the difference that its abolition would make to both the reach of the criminal law and its practical operation. We consider the outcome of these consultations below.[34]

B.   A GENERAL REVIEW OF DISHONESTY OFFENCES

1.16   As we announced in November 1994, it is our intention to embark on a comprehensive review of offences of dishonesty, including those created by the Theft Acts 1968 and 1978. The decision to carry out such a review has been prompted by a number of factors. There has been cogent judicial criticism[35] that "the law of theft is in urgent need of simplification and modernisation". It is also pertinent that in the period since the Theft Act 1968 and the Forgery and Counterfeiting Act 1981 were passed, there have been radical and multifarious advances in the use of modern technology. In consequence, it is likely that certain acts of dishonesty might not be effectively covered by the present legislation. Parliament could not have envisaged all the technical advances and the ensuing problems with which the courts are now concerned. For example the Jack Committee on Banking Services[36] drew attention to various acts of dishonesty which were not covered by the existing legislation.[37] Our present survey has also disclosed other substantial lacunae in the present law, as is apparent from Part IV below.

---

[34]   See Parts IV and V.

[35]   In *Hallam*, *The Times* 27 May 1994 Beldam LJ stated that:

> ... the arguments which occupied a substantial time in the trial court and
> in this court are founded on technicalities which have been grafted on to
> the law of theft since the passing of the Theft Act 1968. That Act itself
> was passed to reform and simplify the law of larceny which had, similarly,
> become over-complicated. Once again the law of theft is in urgent need
> of simplification and modernisation, so that a jury of twelve ordinary
> citizens do not have to grapple with concepts couched in the antiquated
> "franglais" of "choses in action", and scarce public resources of time and
> money are not devoted to hours of semantic argument divorced from the
> true merits of the case. We hope those whose responsibility it is to
> consider reform of the law will have regard to the kind of technicalities
> which have occupied the court, not only in this case but in other cases
> heard in the last two weeks, and will produce a simplified law which
> juries can more readily understand.

[36]   Banking Services: Law and Practice - Report by the Review Committee (1989) Cm 622.

[37]   The Committee pointed out (at para 11.19) that s 5(5) of the Forgery and Counterfeiting Act 1981, which specifically relates to the possession of certain types of counterfeit payment card (including cheque cards and credit cards) and of equipment for manufacturing them, does not extend to debit cards, charge cards, store cards or "any new types of payment yet to be devised", and recommended that the subsection should be amended so that it applied to all payment cards generically. The Committee further recommended the creation of a specific offence of possessing (or selling), with intent to defraud, information that could be used in the manufacture of counterfeit payment cards. The Committee went on to raise (at para 11.21) the question of the use abroad of a counterfeit payment card acquired or manufactured in the United Kingdom.

1.17   We are also very conscious that there has been much criticism of the length and complexity of fraud trials. For example, Lord Alexander of Weedon QC, a former Chairman of the Bar Council and the present Chairman of National Westminster Bank, recently drew attention[38] to problems with serious fraud trials, pointing out that on occasions[39] they were "unfairly protracted, casting long shadows over reputation, and in the end simply failed to do any kind of justice to anyone". He also referred to a recent case[40] in which he was "in no doubt that this very unsatisfactory trial badly dented City confidence in the criminal process". Lord Alexander suggested that, although much of the criticism was directed to the procedure in criminal trials, there was legitimate criticism of the substantive law in substantial fraud cases, which led to trials of excessive length and to perceptions of injustice. We are concerned to discover if it is possible to reduce the length and complexity of trials by simplifying the law, while always ensuring that the defendant is fully protected.

1.18   There is an additional reason why we believe that it is time for a major review. Parliament has imposed upon us the important duty of promoting the codification of the law.[41] From its earliest days, the Commission has seen codification of the criminal law as a central feature of that work; this is an objective that has been achieved in almost all other common law jurisdictions. As we have explained in our last Annual Report,[42] codification is important for two quite different reasons. The criminal law controls the exercise of state power against citizens, and the protection of citizens against unlawful behaviour, and it is important that its rules should be determined by Parliament and not by the sometimes haphazard methods of common law. This can be achieved only if the law is put into statutory form in a comprehensive manner. It is also important from the standpoints of efficiency, economy and the proper administration of justice that the law should be stated in clear and easily accessible terms. The law of dishonesty is obviously of enormous importance in the administration of justice.

1.19   We considered whether to embark on our new dishonesty project without first publishing our final report on conspiracy to defraud. Our clear view is that this report should be published now even though we will have to look at the matter afresh during the course of our forthcoming major review. The size of the dishonesty project and our limited resources mean that it will inevitably take a number of years to complete that work. It is clear from the enquiries that we receive that there is a

---

[38]   In an address to the Commercial Bar Association on 15 June 1994.

[39]   As in the Blue Arrow trial, which started in February 1991 and in which the jury retired exactly one year later.

[40]   The trial of Roger Levitt in November 1993.

[41]   Law Commissions Act 1965, s 3(1).

[42]   Twenty-Eighth Annual Report 1993 (1994) Law Com No 223, HC 341, para 2.27.

wish for us to indicate our present views on conspiracy to defraud as soon as reasonably possible. We also expect that the work that we have done in preparing this report will be of value to us in our dishonesty project, and in particular in looking at the lacunae in the present criminal legal system and the reforms that should be made to remedy them.[43]

C. SUMMARY OF OUR CONCLUSIONS

1.20 We believe that for practical reasons conspiracy to defraud performs a useful role in the present law of dishonesty, and we have concluded that it should remain intact pending our comprehensive review of the law. We have resolved that it would be inappropriate, at a time when we are about to re-examine the whole scheme of dishonesty offences, to make piecemeal recommendations for reform of other aspects of the law of dishonesty. Exceptionally, however, we make one minor recommendation for reform of the law relating to the dishonest obtaining of loans by deception.

D. THE STRUCTURE OF THE REPORT

1.21 In Part II we outline the scope of conspiracy to defraud. We proceed in Part III to consider various criticisms of the offence. We then consider, first, in Part IV, the part that conspiracy to defraud plays in filling gaps in the scheme of substantive dishonesty offences; and secondly, in Part V, the practical considerations that govern the use of conspiracy to defraud. Appendix A contains a draft Bill designed to clarify the law relating to the obtaining of loans of deception.[44] Appendix B contains an extract from the Eighteenth Report of the CLRC.[45] Appendix C consists of charts of statistics relating to prosecutions for fraud offences tried in the Crown Court from 1982 to 1992. In Appendix D we set out various statutory provisions relating to offences of fraud, deception and computer misuse. finally, we list in Appendix E those who sent us comments on WP 104. They comprised quite a wide range of consultants, including members of the judiciary, legal practitioners, investigating and prosecuting authorities and academic lawyers. We are grateful to all those who assisted us in this way. We also had the advantage of seeing in proof the relevant

---

[43] The existence of the offence of conspiracy to defraud and the inadequacies of the existing offences of dishonesty have an impact on civil proceedings, particularly in cases involving the recovery of money paid away in breach of fiduciary duty. The possibility of prosecution for conspiracy to defraud is frequently raised in such cases (see, for example, *Cowan de Groot Properties Ltd v Eagle Trust plc* [1992] 4 All ER 700) and is an issue of considerable concern to practitioners. The defence is not available in respect of offences under the Theft Act 1968: see s 31 of that Act. Following consultations, the Lord Chancellor's Department has recommended the abolition of the rule but with appropriate safeguards: see Written Answers, *Hansard* (HC) 17 December 1992, vol 216, col 350.

[44] See paras 4.25-4.33 below.

[45] See para 1.11 above.

chapters of Dr A T H Smith's new book *Property Offences*,[46] and we are grateful to Dr Smith for his co-operation.

---

[46] Sweet & Maxwell, 1994.

PART II
THE SCOPE OF CONSPIRACY
TO DEFRAUD

A. CONSPIRACY

2.1   The essence of conspiracy, both at common law and under the Criminal Law Act 1977, is agreement. The offence is complete when the agreement is made; it is immaterial that nothing is done to implement the conspiracy or that what is done is different from what was agreed.[1] The prosecution need not, however, identify any party to the conspiracy other than the defendant (hereafter "D"), and he or she may be charged with conspiring with another or others unknown.

2.2   In general, the rules determining what constitutes an agreement for the purpose of conspiracy at common law are similar to those relating to statutory conspiracy.[2] There is, however, one significant difference, which we consider below.[3]

B. THE MEANING OF "DEFRAUD"
1. Economic loss

2.3   The leading case is *Scott*,[4] in which the House of Lords, rejecting an argument that deception was an essential element of conspiracy to defraud,[5] defined the offence in the following terms:

> an agreement by two or more by dishonesty to deprive a person of something which is his or to which he is or would be or might be entitled and an agreement by two or more by dishonesty to injure some proprietary right [of the victim's].[6]

---

[1]   *Bolton* (1992) 94 Cr App R 74, 79-80.

[2]   The 1977 Act, s 2(2), excludes agreements to which the only parties are husband and wife. Although we are unaware of direct authority on the point, this is universally stated to be the law by the authors of treatises and textbooks, and is supported by old authorities (eg *Robinson* (1746) 1 Leach 37; *Whitehouse* (1852) 6 Cox CC 38). It is also supported by a modern Privy Council decision, *Mawji* [1957] AC 126. Section 2(2) of the 1977 Act further excludes liability in the case of a "person under the age of criminal responsibility" (which at present is ten years). We are unaware of any common law authority on the matter; but it has little practical significance in the context of conspiracy to defraud. The third category excluded by the subsection, namely an intended victim, has no relevance to fraud.

[3]   See para 2.13.

[4]   *Scott v Metropolitan Police Commissioner* [1975] AC 819.

[5]   The argument was based on the well-known dictum of Buckley J in *Re London and Globe Finance Corporation Ltd* [1903] 1 Ch 728, 733, that "to defraud is by deceit to induce a course of action". In *Scott*, that definition was held not to be exhaustive.

[6]   *Scott v Metropolitan Police Commissioner* [1975] AC 819, 840F *per* Viscount Dilhorne (with whom the other law lords agreed).

2.4 Although in practice conspiracy to defraud frequently involves the contemplated commission of an offence, it need not do so. One example of conspiracy to defraud where no crime is contemplated is an agreement dishonestly to deprive the victim of possible future profits.[7]

2.5 The *risk* of possible injury to another's right is a sufficient prejudice.[8] Where deception is involved, a person is treated as defrauded if induced to take an economic risk that he would not otherwise have taken[9] or even, it seems, if there is a risk that he may be so induced;[10] it is immaterial that in the event he suffers no loss. A similar principle applies to cases involving no deception.[11]

2. Non-economic loss

2.6 In *Welham*[12] the House of Lords held that the term "defraud" is not confined to causing or taking the risk of causing pecuniary loss to another. In particular, it is fraud to deceive a public official into doing something that he would not have done but for the deceit (or not doing something that but for it he would have done). Lord Denning (with whom the other law lords agreed) stated that it was enough "if anyone may be prejudiced in any way by the fraud".[13] He cited (among other

---

[7] As in *Scott* itself, in which D bribed cinema employees to abstract films, without the consent of their employers or of the copyright owner, for the purpose of making illegal copies and distributing them for profit. Another example is *Cooke* [1986] AC 909; see para 2.10, n 28 below.

[8] "This is of the utmost importance in the criminal law, although it is often overlooked. In many, if not most, large scale company frauds the fraudulent financier never desires, or even foresees that it is probable[,] that loss or injury will be caused to another. He is confident that he will, for example, be able to replace the missing securities by playing the market or bringing some deal to a successful conclusion. The fraud consists in taking a risk of injuring another's right which the accused knows he has no right to take": *Archbold*, vol 2 (1994), para 17-92(iii).

[9] eg *Allsop* (1977) 64 Cr App R 29, 32: "Interests which are imperilled are less valuable in terms of money than those same interests when they are secure and protected." D, a sub-broker for a hire purchase company, in collusion with others entered false particulars on application forms in order to induce the company to accept applications that it might otherwise have rejected. If the debtors met their obligations under the agreements, the hire purchase company would make a profit; but this fact did not negative defrauding, since the debtors constituted a higher risk than the company would normally accept.

[10] It is enough that "the conspirators have dishonestly agreed to bring about a state of affairs which they realise will *or may* deceive the victim into so acting, or failing to act, that he will suffer economic loss or his economic interests will be put at risk": *Wai Yu-tsang* [1992] 1 AC 269, 280A (PC) (emphasis added).

[11] eg *Sinclair* [1968] 1 WLR 1246, in which the directors of a company lent its funds to a third party to enable him to acquire a majority shareholding in the company in return for his promise to transfer to the company assets of equal value.

[12] [1961] AC 103. Although the case concerned the meaning of "intent to defraud" in the Forgery Act 1913 (subsequently repealed and replaced by the Forgery and Counterfeiting Act 1981), the speeches were directed to the meaning of that phrase in general: *Scott* [1975] AC 819, 838 *per* Viscount Dilhorne; *Terry* [1984] AC 374, 381 *per* Lord Fraser of Tullybelton.

[13] *Welham* [1961] AC 103, 133.

instances) the forgery of a doctor's prescription for a drug, notwithstanding that D intended to pay the pharmacist its full price.[14] Similarly, Lord Radcliffe stated that to defraud is to act to the prejudice of another's right, and explained:

> [P]opular speech does not give, and I do not think ever has given, any sure guide as to the limits of what is meant by "to defraud". It may mean to cheat someone. It may mean to practise a fraud upon someone. It may mean to deprive someone by deceit of something which is regarded as belonging to him or, though not belonging to him, as due to him or his right. ... There is nothing in any of this that suggests that to defraud is in ordinary speech confined to the idea of depriving a man by deceit of some economic advantage or inflicting upon him some economic loss.
>
> Has the law ever so confined it? In my opinion there is no warrant for saying that it has.[15]

2.7 The decision of the Court of Appeal in *Moses*[16] provides a recent illustration of the use of conspiracy to defraud to deal with an agreement to deceive a public official into acting contrary to his public duty.[17] The defendants conspired to facilitate applications for work permits by immigrants who were barred by a passport stamp from obtaining such permits. The deception consisted in the withholding from departmental supervisors of information about the applicants, which increased the likelihood of a national insurance number being issued to them.

2.8 The extent to which a conspiracy to cause non-economic loss extends beyond this category is unclear. The authorities conflict. Differing judicial views were expressed in the House of Lords in *Withers*.[18] The narrower view, that this type of case was the

---

[14] At p 131.

[15] At p 124.

[16] [1991] Crim LR 617. The defendants' argument appears to have been based on the inappropriate wording of the indictment in relation to the use of certain application forms.

[17] Earlier authorities include, eg, *Board of Trade v Owen* [1957] AC 602 (agreement to induce a public official, by deception, to grant an export licence); and *Terry* [1984] AC 374 (the defendant used an excise licence, intending police officers to act on the incorrect assumption that it belonged to his vehicle: his intention to pay the licence fee was immaterial).

[18] [1975] AC 842. The defendants fraudulently obtained confidential information both from bank officials and from public servants. They were charged with conspiracy to effect a public mischief, an offence which the House of Lords held to be not known to the law. Viscount Dilhorne (at p 860G) was not prepared to rule out the possibility that a charge of conspiracy to defraud would have lain in respect of the deception of the bank officials (as well as of the public officers); and Lord Reid concurred with him. Lord Diplock (at p 862F-G), Lord Simon of Glaisdale (at p 873B-C) and Lord Kilbrandon (at pp 877G-878A) expressed a contrary view.

only form of non-economic loss covered by conspiracy to defraud, was also expressed by Lord Diplock in *Scott*.[19] The wide views expressed in *Welham*[20] by Lord Radcliffe and Lord Denning were specifically approved by the Privy Council in *Wai Yu-tsang*,[21] in which Lord Goff of Chieveley, who delivered the Board's opinion, said that the cases concerned with public duties did not comprise a special category, but merely exemplified the general principle that conspiracy to defraud need not involve an intention to cause economic loss. Those cases were, Lord Goff explained:[22]

> [o]n the contrary, ... to be understood in the broad sense described by Lord Radcliffe and Lord Denning in *Welham* ... —the view which Viscount Dilhorne favoured in ... *Scott* ..., as apparently did the other members of the Appellate Committee who agreed with him in that case (apart, it seems, from Lord Diplock).[23]

C.   THE CONSPIRATORS' "TRUE OBJECT"

2.9   In *Attorney-General's Reference (No 1 of 1982)*[24] the Court of Appeal held that there was no conspiracy to defraud a company if it would sustain damage only as a "side effect or incidental consequence" of the fraudulent scheme; the defendants did not conspire to defraud the company unless it was their "true object" to inflict such damage.[25]

---

[19] [1975] AC 819, 841B-C. Viscount Dilhorne, who gave the only other detailed speech and with whom Lord Reid, Lord Simon of Glaisdale and Lord Kilbrandon concurred, was less categorical than Lord Diplock. Viscount Dilhorne referred (at p 839C) to Lord Radcliffe's reference in *Welham* "to a special line of cases where the person deceived is a person holding public office or a public authority"; he continued:

> In this case it is not necessary to decide that a conspiracy to defraud may exist even though its object was not to secure a financial advantage by inflicting an economic loss on the person at whom the conspiracy was directed. But for myself I see no reason why what was said by Lord Radcliffe in relation to forgery should not equally apply in relation to conspiracy to defraud.

[20] [1961] AC 103; para 2.6 above.

[21] [1992] 1 AC 269, for the facts of which see para 2.10 below.

[22] [1992] 1 AC 269, 277G.

[23] "This seems to open a very broad vista of potential criminal liability and, if followed, may give a new impetus to the Law Commission's prolonged search for a suitable statutory definition of 'defraud'": Smith and Hogan, *Criminal Law* (7th ed 1992) p 286.

[24] [1983] QB 751.

[25] The defendants planned in England to affix labels of a company to bottles of whisky that did not contain whisky produced by the company. The whisky was to be sold abroad. The court held that the defendants had not conspired to defraud the company but only to obtain money by deception from purchasers of the whisky.

2.10 The term "true object" has not been clearly defined, however; and since in almost every case the conspirators' *purpose* is to make a profit for themselves, the principle is questionable.[26] It is inconsistent with, for example, the Privy Council's approach in *Wai Yu-tsang*.[27] The defendant was the chief accountant of a bank. With the agreement of others, he omitted properly to record dishonoured cheques in the bank's computerised ledgers (though he kept a record in private ledgers). His motive was to try to prevent a run on the bank. It was held that, by intentionally doing an act that he knew might imperil the interests of the bank, he was liable. Delivering the Board's opinion, Lord Goff of Chieveley explained:

> It is however important ... to distinguish a conspirator's intention (or immediate purpose) ... from his motive (or underlying purpose). The latter may be benign in that he does not wish the victim or potential victim to suffer harm; but the mere fact that it is benign will not of itself prevent the agreement from constituting a conspiracy to defraud.[28]

D. DISHONESTY

2.11 Dishonesty is an ingredient of conspiracy to defraud; and although the offence long antedates the Theft Act 1968, "dishonesty" has been held to mean the same in this context as in that Act.[29] In some cases the judge must give the jury a "*Ghosh*"[30] direction—namely, that in determining the issue the jury must decide, first, whether according to the standards of reasonable people what was contemplated was dishonest. If it was, they must decide whether the defendant himself must have realised that what the conspirators planned to do was dishonest by those standards. The test is therefore objective, in the sense that generally accepted standards are

---

[26] "[Fraudsters] act out of greed, not spite. Since they know that they can make a gain only by causing loss or prejudice, they intend to cause the loss or prejudice, even though they have no wish to cause it and perhaps regret the 'necessity' of doing so in order to achieve their object": Smith and Hogan, *Criminal Law* (7th ed 1992) p 286. Similarly, Graham Virgo, "Conspiracy to Defraud—Intent and Prejudice" [1992] CLJ 208, 210:

> A requirement of purpose to defraud is unnecessarily limiting and was
> rightly rejected by the Privy Council [in *Wai Yu-tsang*]. Intention to do
> the acts that will defraud, with proof of dishonesty, should suffice to
> demonstrate culpability, without an additional requirement of foresight of
> a risk of loss.

[27] [1992] 1 AC 269. Although *Attorney-General's Reference* was cited in argument (at p 272C), Lord Goff did not refer to it.

[28] [1992] 1 AC 269, 280A-B. Another example is *Cooke* [1986] AC 909, in which stewards employed by British Rail who sold their own (instead of British Rail) food to customers were held by the House of Lords to be guilty of conspiring to defraud British Rail. The fact that the stewards' *purpose* was to make a profit, not to defraud British Rail, was immaterial. *Attorney-General's Reference* was not cited in *Cooke*.

[29] *Ghosh* [1982] QB 1053, 1059.

[30] *Ibid.*

applied; but also subjective, in the sense that the defendant must realise that the scheme is dishonest on an objective test.

2.12 In many cases, however, a full *Ghosh* direction is unnecessary: "it need only be given where the defendant might have believed that what he is alleged to have done was in accordance with the ordinary person's idea of dishonesty".[31]

E. AGREEMENTS TO ASSIST FRAUD

2.13 In a statutory conspiracy the conspirators must agree that the offence in contemplation will be carried out by one or more of their number.[32] This is not a necessary requirement at common law; so conspiracy to defraud extends to the case in which the parties' purpose is to enable a third party to inflict loss.[33]

F. MODE OF TRIAL AND PENALTY

2.14 Conspiracy to defraud is triable only on indictment. It attracts a maximum penalty (which was formerly at large) of ten years' imprisonment.[34]

G. PROSECUTION GUIDANCE

2.15 There is an important safeguard for defendants in the form of guidance given to prosecutors by the Director of Public Prosecutions as to the circumstances in which it is appropriate to charge conspiracy to defraud rather than substantive offences. The guidance appears in the Code for Crown Prosecutors,[35] which is

---

[31] *Price* (1990) 90 Cr App R 409, 411, following *Roberts* (1987) 84 Cr App R 117. In *Buzalek* [1991] Crim LR 130 (which concerned a charge of fraudulent trading) one of the defendants admitted that he had acted dishonestly in relation to certain transactions, but contended that he had done so in an honest attempt to keep the company going. The trial judge did not give a *Ghosh* direction. The Court of Appeal confirmed that such a direction was unnecessary, since the defendant had confessed at the trial to being dishonest and did not contend that what he did might not have been regarded by others as dishonest. In *Miles* [1992] Crim LR 657 (which also concerned fraudulent trading), the main issue was whether a salesman was, in law, a party to the carrying on of the company's business. The Court of Appeal held that the trial judge need not have gone beyond saying "Dishonesty is at the root of this offence"; and that there had been no need for the judge to give a *Ghosh* direction, since the only issue was whether the defendant knew that certain shares were worthless.

[32] The Criminal Law Act 1977, s 1(1), refers to an agreement to pursue "a course of conduct ... which ... will necessarily amount to or involve the commission of any offence or offences by one or more of the parties to the agreement".

[33] *Hollinshead* [1985] AC 975, considered at paras 4.63-4.68 below. The Court of Appeal, *ibid*, held that an agreement to aid and abet an offence is not a statutory conspiracy to commit an offence. The House of Lords, however, left the question open: [1985] AC 975, 998C-E, *per* Lord Roskill.

[34] Criminal Justice Act 1987, s 12(3). The offence is therefore arrestable (it was originally made arrestable in 1986, by s 24(1) of the Police and Criminal Evidence Act 1984).

[35] Issued pursuant to s 10 of the Prosecution of Offences Act 1985. The Code is laid before Parliament and published (*ibid*, s 9).

a public declaration of the principles upon which the Crown Prosecution Service will exercise its functions. Its purpose is to promote efficient and consistent decision-making so as to develop and thereafter maintain public confidence in the Service's performance of its duties.[36]

2.16 The most recent version of the Code, published in June 1994, is in much less detailed terms than its predecessor and contains no specific reference to conspiracy to defraud. The promulgation of the revised Code does not, however, affect the approach of Crown Prosecutors in deciding whether to charge the offence.[37] The relevant passages in the previous version of the Code were as follows:

15 ... When any substantive offences are no more than steps in the achievement of a dishonest objective, it is open to Crown Prosecutors to concentrate upon that objective and to charge a single count of conspiracy to defraud. It may sometimes be appropriate to charge conspiracy to defraud where the object of the exercise was to swindle a large number of people and a conspiracy to commit a substantive offence is not appropriate and does not meet the justice of the case. Where, however, the essence of the offence is not really fraud at all, as in theft from shops or robbery, it would be wrong to charge conspiracy to defraud relying upon the wide category of offences which might loosely include an element of fraud.

16 The offence is one which juries can readily understand and which enables justice to be done in a class of case which is very injurious to the public at large. It will not normally be appropriate to use it in relation to minor criminal conduct. Crown Prosecutors should always exercise care to ensure that the offence is commensurate with the gravity of the charge.

17 Whether it is appropriate to charge one or other form of conspiracy will depend on the particular facts of the case and trial judges may be expected to intervene to prevent injustices which might otherwise occur. During the course of the trial it may become apparent, for example, that the conspiracy to defraud alleged in the indictment

---

[36] Code for Crown Prosecutors (January 1992), para 1. This passage does not appear in the June 1994 edition: see para 2.16 below.

[37] The Attorney-General stated in a Written Answer, *Hansard* 11 July 1994, vol 246, col 447:

Detailed guidance on particular offences is not appropriate to the revised code and the paragraphs relating to conspiracy to defraud no longer appear. However, the policy and practice of the Crown Prosecution Service in relation to alleged offences of conspiracy to defraud remains unchanged.

could be put more straightforwardly to the jury as a case of obtaining by deception. It may be anticipated that the judge will not hesitate to direct the prosecution to follow that course and will also withdraw from the jury a charge of conspiracy to defraud where he considers it to be oppressive.

H.   OTHER PROCEDURAL SAFEGUARDS

2.17 The power of the trial judge to intervene, referred to in the last paragraph of this passage from the Code for Crown Prosecutors, was explained by the CLRC[38] in the following terms:

> As the evidence emerges at trial, it may for instance become apparent that an alleged conspiracy to defraud could be put more simply to the jury as a case of obtaining property by deception. In such a case ... it would be right for the judge, in the exercise of his inherent jurisdiction to control the proceedings, to direct the prosecution that they should adopt that course so as to ensure that the defendant gets a fair trial. Or where the essence of the conspiracy amounted to an offence or series of offences carrying small penalties it might be appropriate for the judge to say that a charge of conspiracy to defraud would appear to be oppressive.[39]

2.18 Moreover, there are safeguards intended to ensure that the defendant has adequate details of the charges against him. The Court of Appeal held in *Landy*[40] that care must be taken that an indictment for conspiracy to defraud does not lack particularity, in order that (i) the defence and the judge may know precisely, on the face of the indictment itself, the nature of the prosecution's case and (ii) the prosecution cannot shift its ground during the trial without leave of the judge and the making of an amendment. The judge also has a statutory power, in cases of serious and complex fraud, to order a preparatory hearing,[41] at which he may order, among other things, that the prosecution should file a "case statement".[42]

---

[38] See para 1.11 above.

[39] Eighteenth Report (1986), Cmnd 9873, para 4.7. The Report is considered generally at para 1.11 above.

[40] [1981] 1 WLR 355.

[41] Criminal Justice Act 1987, s 7(1). The purposes of the hearing are to identify the material issues; to assist the jury's comprehension of those issues; to expedite proceedings before the jury; or to assist the judge's management of the trial.

[42] The contents of a case statement include the principal facts of the prosecution case, the witnesses who will speak to those facts and any proposition of law on which the prosecution relies: 1987 Act, s 9(4)(a).

I. TERRITORIAL JURISDICTION

1. General

2.19 The present common law rules of territorial jurisdiction relating to conspiracy to defraud, and to a wide range of substantive and other inchoate offences of fraud or dishonesty, will be extended by Part I of the Criminal Justice Act 1993 when that Part of the Act is brought into force.

2. The present law

2.20 A conspiracy to defraud in England and Wales is triable here, wherever the conspiracy is formed;[43] but the English courts have no jurisdiction to try a conspiracy (even if formed here) to defraud outside England and Wales.[44]

3. Part I of the Criminal Justice Act 1993

2.21 As regards conspiracy to defraud here, the present rule is placed on a statutory footing.[45]

2.22 The Act also confers on the courts jurisdiction in some circumstances over a conspiracy to defraud outside England and Wales: *every* party to such a conspiracy becomes triable here if in England and Wales *any* party to it (whether personally or through an agent) (i) did anything to bring it about; (ii) became a party to it; or (iii) did anything to further it.[46] The contemplated fraud must, however, constitute an offence under the law of the place where it is intended to take place.[47]

J. STATISTICS

2.23 Appendix C contains charts showing the number of persons sent for trial for fraud offences in the Crown Court from 1982 to 1992. The fraud offence which is most frequently resorted to is the offence of obtaining property by deception contrary to section 15 of the Theft Act 1968; in 1992, for example, 3732 out of 5434 (69%) defendants sent for trial in the Crown Court on fraud offences were charged with that offence. Conspiracy to defraud was the next most frequently charged offence. It seems possible that the charts reflect the effect both of *Ayres*[48] and of its subsequent statutory reversal.[49] Whereas in 1983, 956 persons were sent for trial for

---

[43]   *Sansom* [1991] 2 QB 130; *Liangsiriprasert v United States* [1991] AC 225.

[44]   *Board of Trade v Owen* [1957] AC 602; *Attorney-General's Reference (No 1 of 1982)* [1983] QB 751, para 2.9 above.

[45]   1993 Act, s 3(2).

[46]   1993 Act, s 5(3).

[47]   1993 Act, s 6. This requirement is presumed to be satisfied unless, by notice, the defendant puts the prosecution to proof within such time as may be prescribed by rules of court.

[48]   [1984] AC 447; see para 1.8 above.

[49]   By the Criminal Justice Act 1987, s 12(1); see para 1.11 above.

conspiracy to defraud, by 1987 the equivalent figure was 199; and there was a more or less corresponding increase in the number of those who were sent for trial on charges of obtaining by deception. Conversely, by 1992 the number of those sent for trial charged with conspiracy to defraud had increased to 508 and there was a decrease in the number of those charged with obtaining by deception.

2.24 So far as the length and type of sentences are concerned, the figures are not separately recorded in the Criminal Statistics for each offence. However, figures were obtained from the Home Office for 1992, which showed that of the 353 defendants who were found guilty of conspiracy to defraud, 174 were given a sentence of immediate custody, 94 a fully suspended sentence and 85 were otherwise dealt with.

PART III
CRITICISMS OF CONSPIRACY
TO DEFRAUD

A.   GENERAL

3.1   In WP 104[1] we considered a number of well-known objections of principle to the continuing existence of the offence of conspiracy to defraud. We return now to those criticisms in the light of the comments on them that we received on consultation,[2] the subsequent enquiries to which we refer in paragraphs 1.14 and 1.15 above, and recent decisions.

B.   THE OFFENCE APPLIES TO AGREEMENTS TO DO LAWFUL ACTS

3.2   The first objection to conspiracy to defraud is that it runs counter to the principle established, in accordance with our recommendations,[3] in section 1 of the Criminal Law Act 1977—namely, that an act should not be criminal *merely* because more than one person is involved.[4] Before 1977, an agreement to do an "unlawful", though not criminal, act could amount to a criminal conspiracy, as could an agreement to do a lawful act by unlawful means.

3.3   Our recommendation that the object of a conspiracy should be limited to the commission of a substantive offence was originally put forward, "very emphatically",[5] as a provisional proposal in a working paper published in 1973.[6] The proposal met with a very wide measure of approval on consultation.[7] Conspiracy to defraud was retained, also in accordance with our recommendation,[8] as a temporary exception pending completion of a consideration of the extent of the offences which would be required in its place.

---

[1]   See para 1.12 above.

[2]   In Part IV, below, we refer further to the response on consultation during our consideration of some of the possible gaps in the law that would arise if conspiracy to defraud were abolished.

[3]   For these recommendations, see Criminal Law: Conspiracy and Criminal Law Reform (1976) Law Com No 76, HC 176, para 7.2.

[4]   Except of course where an offence (such as riot or violent disorder under the Public Order Act 1986, ss 1 and 2) is so formulated as to require the participation of more than one offender. The essence of this type of offence is the presence of a particular number of people, and the greater danger of violent acts being done in their presence.

[5]   See Law Com No 76, para 1.9.

[6]   Inchoate Offences, Working Paper No 50, paras 8-14; see para 1.3 above. The relevant passages are cited in full in Law Com No 76, para 1.8.

[7]   Law Com No 76, para 1.9.

[8]   Law Com No 76, para 1.16.

3.4 Many serious frauds involve more than one person, and the fact that a number of people are involved may be an aggravating factor. As Professor Sir John Smith has suggested,[9] although it is "of course illogical" to provide that it is an offence to conspire to do something which is not an offence,

> it is arguable that the requirement of conspiracy provides a desirable constraint on what would otherwise be too wide-ranging an offence. Few would want to make a criminal of the person who quite deliberately defers payment of his gas bill until he gets the threatening red reminder, even though he knows perfectly well that he is causing an unjustifiable loss to the Gas Board; but ... company directors ... who decide as a matter of policy to defer payment of their suppliers for long periods, being well aware of the damage they are doing, seem to fall into a quite different category. Of course, it is not only the fact of agreement which makes the conduct so serious—an individual in a large way of business might do the same—but it is a significant fact. Where there is no agreement the matter is likely to be trivial and the line between negligence and intention will be hard to draw. Where there is agreement, it is clearly intentional and likely to be substantial.[10]

3.5 It remains true, none the less, that the existence of an agreement may be only one of a number of possible aggravating factors against which the seriousness of the criminal conduct is to be measured. Aggravating factors such as this usually affect the length or type of sentence rather than the issue of liability. To put the instant objection the other way: why should the absence of this particular aggravating factor mean that in some cases there should be no criminal liability at all?

3.6 We entirely accept that, as a matter of principle, this argument is valid; and that *either* it should be an offence to defraud *or* it should not be an offence for two or more persons to agree to do so. We explain below[11] why we are unable, however, to recommend either option in the context of this report.

C. THE WIDTH OF THE OFFENCE

3.7 A second objection of principle to conspiracy to defraud is that the offence is too wide. There are two aspects to this objection. The first is that the offence is too wide because of its overlap with statutory conspiracy and with substantive offences, such as theft and obtaining by deception. We consider this in the following

---

[9] In a paper delivered at a seminar on "Pressing Problems in the Law: Fraud and the Criminal Law", held at All Souls College, Oxford on 2 July 1994 under the aegis of the Society of Public Teachers of Law. The papers given at the seminar will in due course be published under the same title.

[10] *Ibid*, p 18.

[11] In Parts IV and V.

paragraphs. The second aspect is that it is too wide because the very broad scope of the offence means that it covers certain conduct which arguably ought not to be criminal at all. We consider this aspect in Part IV below. On consultation there was no clear preponderance of opinion among respondents on the question whether, in either respect, the width of the offence was excessive.

3.8 Conduct sufficient to found conspiracy to defraud embraces almost every offence in the Theft Acts.[12] In principle (the objection runs), overlapping offences should be avoided unless there is some reason which makes the overlap acceptable; and the objection is stronger where there is not merely an overlap but a total subsumption of other offences. Arguably, it allows too much discretion to prosecutors as to which charge to bring where either charge would be possible, but where only one of them is desirable in the circumstances.

3.9 The problem of overlap is not, however, confined to conspiracy to defraud. In particular, the effect of the recent decision of the House of Lords in *Gomez*[13] is that almost every offence of obtaining property by deception automatically amounts also to theft.[14] The question of overlap generally, and not only in relation to conspiracy to defraud, will fall for consideration in our forthcoming review of dishonesty offences. It should be borne in mind that, meanwhile, there are safeguards against injustice to defendants that may arise from an oppressive use of conspiracy to defraud.[15]

D.   THE VAGUE AND UNCERTAIN SCOPE OF THE OFFENCE

3.10 Another objection to conspiracy to defraud which may therefore be raised is that the boundaries of the offence are uncertain; that it offers insufficient guidance as to what can or cannot lawfully be done; and that it consequently infringes the principle that it should be possible to ascertain in advance whether any particular conduct would be criminal.[16] On this view, the criminal law should have no place for an offence

---

[12]   See, eg, *Scott* [1975] AC 819; para 2.3 above.

[13]   [1993] AC 442.

[14]   This follows from the ruling of the House that the owner's consent is immaterial to the issue whether property has been "appropriated" for the purpose of theft. Exceptionally, land can be obtained by deception but (with limited exceptions) it cannot be stolen: Theft Act 1968, s 4(2); *Gomez* [1993] AC 442, 496 *per* Lord Browne-Wilkinson.

[15]   See paras 2.17-2.18 above.

[16]   A particular aspect of the present criticism of conspiracy to defraud is sometimes expressed as "dishonesty does all the work". See, eg, Glanville Williams, *Textbook of Criminal Law* (2nd ed 1983) p 708:

> For theft you must appropriate property belonging to another, etc.;
> for obtaining you must obtain property by deception, etc. The
> requirement of dishonesty is an extra. In the case of conspiracy to
> defraud there appears to be no other requirement, apart from the
> agreement. Anything that the jury labels (and is allowed to label)
> as dishonest becomes punishable as the object of a conspiracy to

which is not sufficiently precise that it is possible to say with reasonable certainty whether any combination of facts constitutes the offence.[17]

3.11   We have consistently favoured this approach. In a different context,[18] we have said:

> Since 1973 the working papers and reports we have published have returned repeatedly to [the] theme that the criminal law must be both certain and accessible, and it has received widespread endorsement from those who have responded to our working papers. Thus in 1973 we said that it seemed to us not merely desirable, but obligatory, that legal rules imposing serious criminal sanctions should be stated with the maximum clarity that the imperfect medium of language could attain.[19] The following year we repeated this principle in another Working Paper when we said that if legislation did not cover every kind of previously unidentified wicked conduct this was the inevitable price which had to be paid for an acceptable degree of certainty as to the conduct to be penalised by the law.[20] Our view that this price was one which we believed to be worth paying was one which was supported by most of those who responded to that paper.[21] When we were concerned with the task of codifying the old common law offences in the field of public order we said that a criminal code must define with precision what conduct it is which is a crime.[22] And when we published our report on a Criminal Code[23] we reiterated our view that codification of the criminal law was desirable not only as a matter of constitutional principle but also because it offered instrumental benefits in the way of

---

[17]   defraud. This is too vague a test to serve as the foundation of criminal liability.

In WP 104, para 5.9, we rejected a possible argument that unfairness in the generality of the offence could be offset by giving the defendant particulars of the case he had to answer. This argument, we pointed out, confused two issues:

> The principle *nulla poena sine lege* is intended to ensure that a person may ascertain in advance whether or not his conduct would, if proved, amount to an offence. Particulars, on the other hand, are to help the defendant meet the allegations of fact brought in support of the charge.

[18]   Binding Over (1994) Law Com No 222, Cm 2439, para 4.12; footnotes in original.

[19]   Working Paper No 50 (1973) para 9.

[20]   Working Paper No 57 (1974) para 44.

[21]   Law Com No 76 (1976) para 3.18.

[22]   Working Paper No 82 (1982) para 3.1.

[23]   Law Com No 177 (1989).

greater accessibility, comprehensibility, consistency and certainty. This view was again strongly supported by those we consulted.[24]

3.12 On the other hand, it may well be asked: if a person inflicts loss on another *knowing* that his conduct would be regarded as dishonest by the ordinary standards of reasonable and honest people,[25] does he have a legitimate complaint if he is prosecuted for his behaviour? Moreover, in the light of *Gomez*,[26] dishonesty now does all the work in many cases of theft: the absence of dishonesty is, for example, the only reason why a shopper in a supermarket does not steal goods by removing them from the shelf. This will be one of the many issues examined in our review of dishonesty offences.

3.13 Although some aspects of conspiracy to defraud are undoubtedly vague in principle, on consultation we received little comment directed to the instant point; and while, of those few who did comment, some endorsed this criticism, the Serious Fraud Office did not accept that the offence is so uncertain as to be capable of covering conduct that should not be treated as criminal.[27]

E. THE MAXIMUM PENALTY FOR THE OFFENCE

3.14 Before the Criminal Law Act 1977 the penalty for conspiracy was at large. Section 3(2) and (3) of the Act limited the maximum penalty for a conspiracy to commit an offence to that for the offence itself; and this principle applies even where the conspiracy consisted of an agreement to commit a number of offences.[28] In the Report[29] on which the Act was based, the Commission abandoned its original proposal (which met with almost universal disapproval on consultation) that, where a conspiracy to commit more than one indictable offence of the same nature was established, the maximum penalty should be twice that provided for the substantive offence. The Commission explained in the Report:

> If more than one substantive indictable offence is actually committed, then they are charged separately and the legal maximum penalty which can be imposed is multiplied by the number of substantive offences of which any defendant is convicted; sentences of imprisonment can be made consecutive. If conspiracy charges are only used in cases where

---

[24] *Ibid*, para 2.12.

[25] *Ghosh* [1982] QB 1053; see para 2.11 above.

[26] For which see para 3.9 above.

[27] Cf para 3.7 above.

[28] If a conspiracy involves two or more contemplated offences which have different maximum sentences, the longer (or longest) sentence is the maximum for the conspiracy.

[29] Criminal Law: Conspiracy and Criminal Law Reform (1976) Law Com No 76, paras 1.98-1.100.

the substantive offences have not been consummated, which in general we believe should be the case,[30] then we think that the maximum for one substantive offence is entirely adequate.[31]

3.15 We stated in WP 104:

> Conspiracy to defraud subsumes a wide range of substantive offences. In some cases the maximum penalty for the substantive offence is the same as that which is now provided for conspiracy to defraud, namely ten years' imprisonment;[32] in other cases the maximum penalty for the substantive offence will be significantly lower. The force of the objection to the existence of a higher maximum penalty for conspiracy to defraud than would be available for a statutory conspiracy to commit the substantive offence is less strong now that the maximum for the former is no longer at large, but the objection of principle remains to be answered.[33]

3.16 There is, however, a significant distinction in this respect between conspiracy to defraud and a conspiracy to commit an offence. Where the parties to a statutory conspiracy have carried out their scheme, they are not normally charged with conspiracy as well.[34] On the other hand, whether or not the plan of conspirators to defraud has succeeded, they can be convicted only of conspiracy. Since the purpose of fraudsters is usually to make an illicit profit, arguably there are cases where the profit is so substantial that, coupled with the other circumstances of the case, a long term of imprisonment may be required. The high maximum penalty gives the sentencer no greater discretion than he would have in the case of a conviction in the Crown Court for obtaining by deception, an offence which may involve facts ranging from the trivial to the very serious.

3.17 On consultation, the question of sentence appears not to have greatly troubled commentators, few of whom commented expressly on this point. His Honour Judge Michael Coombe, one of those who did express a view, suggested that multiple participation in a complex fraud added to the seriousness of the offence, and that

---

[30] See para 3.16, n 34 below.

[31] Law Com No 76, para 1.100 (footnote added).

[32] Criminal Justice Act 1987, s 12(3).

[33] WP 104, para 5.11 (footnote added).

[34] Under a Practice Direction (*Practice Direction (Crime: Conspiracy)* [1977] 1 WLR 537), if substantive counts and a related conspiracy count are joined in the indictment, the prosecution must elect to proceed either on the substantive counts or on the conspiracy count (unless, in the interests of justice, the judge directs otherwise). So where a conspiracy count adds nothing to the charge of a substantive offence, it has no place in the indictment: *Jones* (1974) 59 Cr App R 120.

the severity of the maximum penalty had the advantage of avoiding the need for consecutive sentences which would be required if a conspirator had to be charged with, and was convicted of, a number of discrete offences comprised in the conspiracy. We see considerable force in what he says.

PART IV
CONDUCT THAT WOULD CEASE TO BE CRIMINAL IF CONSPIRACY TO DEFRAUD WERE ABOLISHED

A.   GENERAL

4.1   The offence of conspiracy to defraud is so widely defined that certain kinds of conduct are capable of falling within it (provided the element of conspiracy is present, and subject to the issue of dishonesty) although they amount to no substantive offence or it is doubtful whether they do so. If the offence were abolished these kinds of conduct would, or might, cease to be criminal altogether. In Part IV of WP 104 we attempted to identify them, and referred to them as possible "gaps" in the law. Our use of this term was not of course intended to imply that they *should* continue to be criminal: that is a separate issue. On the contrary, we recognise that the existence of such potential "gaps" can logically be regarded as a reason either for retaining the offence or for abolishing it, depending on one's point of view. But we would make two general points.

4.2   First, in the case of certain kinds of conduct in this category there is no general agreement whether they ought to be criminal. Ordinarily we would consider the arguments for and against imposing criminal liability in each such case, and express our concluded view. As we have already explained, however, we are about to embark on a major review of the law of dishonesty which will include, but go far beyond, the particular areas in question. It will look at all the major offences of dishonesty and consider whether reforms are desirable. If we were to attempt to form a view on the disputed areas at this stage, any such view would certainly have to be reconsidered, and might have to be revised, in the course of our dishonesty project. In particular, that review may well lead us to recommend the creation of new offences, so that we cannot now identify any possible gaps that would remain. In the circumstances we have concluded that it would be inappropriate and premature for us to attempt to resolve these issues in the present report.

4.3   Secondly, some of these kinds of conduct are *not* controversial: it is widely accepted that they *ought* to be criminal,[1] and that, if conspiracy to defraud is the only offence that catches them, that is a defect not of conspiracy to defraud but of the law of dishonesty in general. It follows that the simple abolition of conspiracy to defraud, without replacement, would leave not just "gaps" in the law but *undesirable* gaps; and we therefore do not recommend that course. Moreover, for the reasons given in the previous paragraph we are not yet in a position to recommend such extensions of the substantive law of dishonesty as would catch these kinds of conduct, and would thus meet this objection to the abolition of the offence.

---

[1]   Clearly there is no conduct caught by conspiracy to defraud which it is agreed ought *not* to be criminal.

4.4 It follows that the existence of kinds of conduct which can amount to conspiracy to defraud, but which arguably amount to no other offence—whether or not it be generally agreed that they *should* amount to another offence—makes it impossible for us to recommend the immediate abolition of conspiracy to defraud without its replacement by a statutory offence at least as wide. We turn now to make a further attempt to identify the kinds of conduct in question. Comparison with WP 104 will show that there appear to be more of them than were there discussed.

B. SPECIFIC MATTERS

1. Introduction: list of the matters considered

4.5 In this section we consider the following matters:

Property that cannot be stolen.[2]

Confidential information.[3]

The temporary deprivation of property.[4]

Cases in which there is no "property belonging to another".[5]

Secret profits made by employees and fiduciaries.[6]

Obtaining loans by deception.[7]

The obtaining without deception of benefits other than property.[8]

Deception of computers and other machines.[9]

Evasion of liability without intent to make permanent default.[10]

Obtaining by giving a false general impression.[11]

---

[2] See para 4.6 below.

[3] See paras 4.7-4.9 below.

[4] See paras 4.10-4.16 below.

[5] See paras 4.17-4.19 below.

[6] See paras 4.20-4.24 below.

[7] See paras 4.25-4.33 below.

[8] See paras 4.34-4.39 below.

[9] See paras 4.40-4.46 below.

[10] See paras 4.47-4.49 below.

[11] See paras 4.50-4.51 below.

Dishonest failure to pay for goods or services.[12]

Gambling swindles.[13]

Corruption not involving consideration.[14]

"Prejudice" without financial loss.[15]

Assisting in fraud by third parties.[16]

Ignorance of the details of the fraud.[17]

Commercial swindles.[18]

2.   Property that cannot be stolen

4.6   For the purposes of the offences of theft and obtaining property by deception "property" is defined as including "money and all other property, real or personal, including things in action and other intangible property".[19] However, it is further provided that certain kinds of property cannot be stolen, namely land (except in certain circumstances),[20] things growing wild on land (unless picked for commercial purposes)[21] and game (unless reduced into possession by another).[22] An agreement dishonestly to move a fence, thus effectively depriving a neighbouring landowner of part of his land, would not be a conspiracy to steal but would presumably be a conspiracy to defraud. The CLRC considered these kinds of property in detail in 1966[23] and concluded that it should not normally be criminal to appropriate them—a recommendation accepted by Parliament. In WP 104 we expressed the provisional view that in these circumstances it was unnecessary for conspiracy to

---

[12]   See para 4.52 below.

[13]   See paras 4.53-4.55 below.

[14]   See paras 4.56-4.57 below.

[15]   See paras 4.58-4.62 below.

[16]   See paras 4.63-4.68 below.

[17]   See paras 4.69-4.72 below.

[18]   See para 4.73 below.

[19]   Theft Act 1968, s 4(1).

[20]   Theft Act 1968, s 4(2).

[21]   Theft Act 1968, s 4(3).

[22]   Theft Act 1968, s 4(4).

[23]   Criminal Law Revision Committee, Eighth Report, Theft and Related Offences (1966), Cmnd 2977, paras 40-55.

defraud to supplement the law of theft in this respect.[24] In the course of our review of dishonesty we shall need to consider whether these exceptions to the general rule need to be retained. In the meantime we see no reason why, in an appropriate case, a concerted and dishonest appropriation of such property should not be prosecuted as a conspiracy to defraud.

3.   Confidential information

4.7   Information, particularly confidential information, is often a valuable commodity and is sometimes treated by the law as a kind of property;[25] but its peculiar characteristics make it difficult to regard it as property in the strict sense, and it was held in *Oxford v Moss*[26] that a dishonest obtaining of confidential information is therefore not theft. Similarly, no doubt, to obtain it by deception would not amount to the offence of obtaining property by deception.[27] Even if information were to be regarded as "property" within the meaning of the Act, the requirement of an intention permanently to deprive could scarcely be satisfied:

> It is difficult to see how there is any question of deprivation where someone has, in breach of confidence, forced the original holder to share, but not forget, his secret.[28]

4.8   There are, however, a number of offences that might be committed in the course of such conduct. If the information is kept on a physical medium such as paper or computer disks, the dishonest acquisition of that medium can amount to theft or to obtaining property by deception. Unauthorised access to a computer can also be an offence under the Computer Misuse Act 1990.[29] If the information is obtained by deception on the understanding that it has been or will be paid for, there may be an obtaining of services by deception.[30] If the information is obtained by bribery or corruption there may be an offence under the Prevention of Corruption Acts 1889

---

[24]   WP 104, para 4.8, where we expressed the provisional view that the abolition of conspiracy to defraud would call for no change in respect of these matters. We explained (in n 17 to that paragraph) that in WP 56 (see para 1.4 above), para 60, we had reached a similar conclusion, which had been confirmed on consultation.

[25]   eg *Green v Folgham* (1823) 1 Sim & Stu 398; *Exchange Telegraph Co Ltd v Howard* (1906) 22 TLR 375; *Re Keene* [1922] 2 Ch 475.

[26]   (1979) 68 Cr App R 183.

[27]   Theft Act 1968, s 15(1).

[28]   N.E.Palmer and Paul Kohler, "Information as Property", in N.E.Palmer and Ewan McKendrick (eds), *Interests in Goods* (1993) p 203.

[29]   See para 4.42 below. Section 1 of the Act (which provides for the basic offence, "hacking") is set out in Appendix D below.

[30]   Theft Act 1978, s 1(1). But a computer probably cannot be deceived: para 4.40 below.

to 1916.[31] There may be an offence under the Copyright, Designs and Patents Act 1988 of making or dealing with an infringing copy[32] or an illicit recording.[33]

4.9   Finally, if two or more people are involved there might be a conspiracy to defraud: the acquisition of confidential information is clearly an act to the prejudice of the person entitled to it. In some cases this would be the only possible charge. In 1987 we were not aware of the offence being used in such circumstances,[34] but such use is in fact not uncommon—particularly where an employee has somehow been induced to divulge confidential information otherwise than for consideration.[35] We are not convinced that conduct of this kind can be adequately dealt with by the civil law alone:[36] one reason being that if the wrongdoer does not have sufficient assets there is no enforceable or adequate remedy against him. We believe that in some cases such conduct ought to be criminal, and in the absence of conspiracy to defraud would cease to be so. We shall consider the question of confidential information in our forthcoming general review of dishonesty offences.

4.   Temporary deprivation of property

4.10   Where a person dishonestly appropriates property belonging to another without that other's consent, or dishonestly obtains it by deception, he neither steals the property nor commits an offence of obtaining property by deception unless his intention is permanently to deprive the other of the property.[37] The mere borrowing or use of

---

[31]   But cf paras 4.56-4.57 below.

[32]   Section 107.

[33]   Section 198.

[34]   WP 104, para 10.47. On consultation opinion was divided. Those who favoured the application of a criminal sanction to at least some forms of dishonest acquisition of information included: Judge Rant QC; the Inland Revenue; the Serious Fraud Office; the Crown Prosecution Service; British Telecom; the Department of Trade and Industry Insolvency Service; and the Confederation of British Industry. Some of those who expressed this view qualified their support: eg, the Confederation of British Industry would wish any offence to apply only to commercial information. Opponents included the Metropolitan and City Police Company Fraud Department and the Society of Public Teachers of Law, on the ground that the matter was essentially one of civil law. The Criminal Bar Association agreed with our provisional view in WP 104, at para 10.48, that it would be inappropriate to review the question in the present exercise.

[35]   Where consideration is involved, a corruption offence may be available. See paras 4.56-4.57 below.

[36]   As regards the civil law, cf our Report on Breach of Confidence (1981) Law Com No 110, Cmnd 8388, in which we recommended that the existing law of confidence should be replaced by a statutory tort consisting in the unauthorised use or disclosure of information that was subject to an obligation of confidence. We further recommended that such an obligation should arise where information had been given to a person on his express or implied undertaking not to use or disclose it except as authorised; or where the information was obtained by any of several "improper" means. The obligation would also bind a third party into whose hands the information subsequently came as soon as he became aware that the information was "impressed" with an obligation of confidence.

[37]   Theft Act 1968, s 1(1) (theft); s 15(1) (obtaining property by deception). Sections 1 and

another's property will not suffice, even if unauthorised (or authorised only as a result of deception) and even if it results in loss to the owner—for example, because he is deprived of the opportunity to derive financial advantage from using the property for his own purposes.

4.11   This rule is qualified in several ways. First, in the case of certain kinds of property (namely conveyances[38] and articles on display in places open to the public)[39] even a temporary taking, if unauthorised, will amount to a specific offence.

4.12   Secondly, a temporary obtaining of property by deception may amount to the offence of obtaining *services* by deception,[40] but only if the benefit thus conferred is conferred "on the understanding that the benefit has been or will be paid for". If it is *not* conferred on that understanding, because the defendant has by deception obtained exemption from the need to pay, there may be an offence of obtaining by deception an *exemption* from liability to make a payment.[41] (If the defendant by deception obtains a *reduction* in the price that would normally be chargeable it would appear that he may be guilty both of obtaining services and of obtaining an *abatement* of liability to make a payment.)[42]

4.13   Thirdly, a person who is required or expected to pay "on the spot" for any "goods supplied or service done" (which presumably includes the use of property), and dishonestly makes off without paying, may be guilty of an offence[43] if his intention is *never* to pay.[44]

4.14   Fourthly, if a borrowing or lending of property is "for a period or in circumstances making it equivalent to an outright taking or disposal" it may be *deemed* to have been done with an intention permanently to deprive,[45] so that a conviction for theft or obtaining property by deception may be possible.

4.15   However, there are certainly cases of dishonest borrowing or use which will not necessarily amount to any substantive offence: one example is the unauthorised use by employees of their employers' premises and equipment for their own profit. It

---

15 are set out in Appendix D below.

[38]   Theft Act 1968, s 12.

[39]   Theft Act 1968, s 11.

[40]   Theft Act 1978, s 1(1).

[41]   Theft Act 1978, s 2(1)(c).

[42]   *Ibid.*

[43]   Theft Act 1978, s 3(1).

[44]   *Allen* [1985] AC 1029.

[45]   Theft Act 1968, s 6(1).

seems clear that the definition of fraud laid down in *Scott*[46] is wide enough to cover conduct of this kind.[47] *Scott* itself was concerned with an agreement to borrow films from a cinema, without authority, for the purpose of making copies: the real loss was sustained by the owners of the copyright and the distribution rights, but the decision would presumably have been the same had the conspirators' purpose been to deprive the cinema owners of a day's takings.[48]

4.16　Whether *all* such conduct ought to be criminal is debatable: it has been argued that it should be brought within the scope of theft.[49] This is a matter we will have to decide in the course of our review of offences of dishonesty. But we think that there are *some* cases of temporary deprivation which ought to be criminal, which are now criminal if done in pursuance of an agreement, and which would cease to be criminal if conspiracy to defraud were abolished without replacement.

5.　No property "belonging to another"

4.17　In some cases a defendant has dealt with property in his possession in a way which many would regard as dishonest, but he may have committed no substantive offence because the property in question does not "belong to another" within the meaning of the Theft Act 1968. Technically he has not infringed another's proprietary rights: he has merely failed to satisfy a personal obligation.

4.18　An example is *Lewis v Lethbridge*,[50] where the defendant had appropriated a sum of money which he had collected from sponsors for charity. His conviction for theft was quashed because it did not appear that he was under any obligation to hand over the actual cash he received from the sponsors, or to keep the money separate from his own.[51]

4.19　Another example is *Clowes (No 2)*,[52] where one of the defendants was convicted of stealing large sums of money entrusted by investors to his company for investment in Government stocks. The convictions were upheld only after much learned argument as to whether the company was a trustee of the funds invested or only a

---

[46]　[1975] AC 819; para 2.3 above.

[47]　Smith and Hogan, *Criminal Law* (7th ed 1992) p 285.

[48]　There would still have been no property *belonging to the cinema owners* of which they were permanently deprived.

[49]　Glanville Williams, "Temporary Appropriation should be Theft" [1981] Crim LR 129. See WP 104, Part XIII.

[50]　[1987] Crim LR 59.

[51]　Cf Theft Act 1968, s 5(3).

[52]　[1994] 2 All ER 316.

debtor, in which case the funds would not be property "belonging to another".[53] Had the Court of Appeal taken the opposite view, as it might well have done, we have no doubt that there would have been calls for an urgent review of this area of the law. We think it arguable that the offence of theft is too narrowly drawn in this respect;[54] but if it is, the defect is in some cases[55] already remediable by resort to conspiracy to defraud. A dishonest agreement that a debtor will spend the money he has borrowed, knowing that this will make it impossible for him to repay the debt, is clearly capable of amounting to a conspiracy to defraud: it is an agreement "to deprive a person of something ... to which he is or would be or might be entitled".[56]

6. Secret profits by employees and fiduciaries

4.20 A variation of the problem arising where there is no property "belonging to another" is that of the fiduciary who abuses his position so as to make a secret profit for which he dishonestly omits to account. In *Attorney-General's Reference (No 1 of 1985)*[57] the Court of Appeal held that such a person does not thereby steal the proceeds, because they do not belong to another: his beneficiary has no "proprietary right or interest"[58] in them, and he does not receive them on his beneficiary's account.[59] Thus the manager of a public house did not commit theft by selling his own beer, in breach of his duty to his employers, and keeping the profits. However, in *Cooke*[60] it was held by the House of Lords, on essentially similar facts,[61] that there was a conspiracy to defraud.[62]

---

[53] Jonathan S. Fisher, "Naylor and Clowes: A Prosecution which Nearly Foundered on the Rocks of Trust Law" [1994] JIBL 212.

[54] The contrary view is that a person who has no *obligation* to keep property separate from his own ought not to be treated as stealing the property, since he has not appropriated property belonging to another. Even if dishonest he is, in other words, a debtor rather than a thief.

[55] Though not in *Clowes (No 2)*, where there was insufficient evidence of conspiracy.

[56] *Scott* [1975] AC 819, 840, *per* Viscount Dilhorne.

[57] [1986] QB 491.

[58] Theft Act 1968, s 5(1).

[59] Theft Act 1968, s 5(3).

[60] [1986] AC 909.

[61] The defendants were railway stewards who had sold their own food and drink to passengers, thus depriving British Rail of the profits. However, the main concern of the House was to distinguish *Ayres* (see para 1.9 above). *Attorney-General's Reference (No 1 of 1982)* [1983] QB 751 (para 2.9 above) was not cited.

[62] In *Tarling v Government of the Republic of Singapore* (1978) 70 Cr App R 77 the House of Lords said that it was not fraudulent for company directors to make secret profits at the expense of their companies; but, with respect, this seems unduly generous.

4.21   Whether this is a case where conspiracy to defraud plugs a gap in the law of theft is, however, no longer clear, because it now appears as a result of a recent Privy Council case[63] that conduct of this kind may after all be theft as well as fraud. In *Attorney-General's Reference (No 1 of 1985)* the court relied upon the civil case of *Lister & Co v Stubbs*[64] as authority for the proposition that the beneficiary has no proprietary interest in the proceeds of the fraud. In that case, an employee received a bribe in the course of conducting his employer's business. The Court of Appeal held that, while the employee was bound to account to his employer for the amount of the bribe, their relationship was that of debtor and creditor, not trustee and beneficiary. On that basis, a bribe or secret profit does not *belong* (even in equity) to the employer and cannot, therefore, found a charge of theft.

4.22   In the recent civil case of *Attorney-General for Hong Kong v Reid*,[65] however, the Privy Council declined to follow *Lister & Co v Stubbs* and held that in these circumstances there *is* a trust. Lord Templeman, who delivered the Board's opinion, stated[66] that *Lister & Co v Stubbs* was "inconsistent with earlier authorities which were not cited" and with

> the principles that a fiduciary must not be allowed to benefit from his own breach of duty, that the fiduciary should account for the bribe as soon as he receives it and that equity regards as done that which ought to be done. From these principles it would appear to follow that the bribe and the property from time to time representing the bribe are held on a constructive trust for the person injured.

4.23   It remains to be seen whether this decision will be followed by the English courts,[67] and if so whether it will be regarded as undermining the reasoning in *Attorney-General's Reference (No 1 of 1985)*. The English courts may take the view that, even if there is a trust as a matter of civil law, to base a conviction for theft on this fact would be to stretch the offence too far.[68] It is therefore still possible that if

---

[63]   *Attorney-General for Hong Kong v Reid* [1994] 1 AC 324; see para 4.22 below.

[64]   (1890) 45 Ch D 1.

[65]   [1994] 1 AC 324. Professor Sir John Smith suggests in a case-note that, if followed by the English courts, the decision substantially extends the law of theft in a way that Parliament did not intend when enacting the 1968 Act: (1994) 110 LQR 180, 183.

[66]   [1994] 1 AC 324, 336F-G.

[67]   There is authority for the view that the Court of Appeal is free to follow a decision of the Privy Council which conflicts with a previous decision of its own: *Worcester Works Finance Ltd v Cooden Engineering Ltd* [1972] 1 QB 210 *per* Lord Denning MR (at p 217E-F) and Phillimore LJ (at p 219A).

[68]   In *Attorney-General's Reference*, the Court of Appeal was asked three questions. The second was:

> On a charge of theft, where an employee has used his employer's

conspiracy to defraud were abolished a dishonest agreement of this kind would cease to be criminal altogether.

4.24   We express no view at present as to whether such an agreement ought to be a conspiracy to *steal*, nor as to whether (in the absence of a wide-ranging offence such as conspiracy to defraud) it would be appropriate to create a specific offence to cover such conduct;[69] but we believe that there are circumstances in which it ought to be criminal, and our consultation revealed a measure of support for this view. This is therefore a potential gap which in our view would be undesirable.

7.   Obtaining loans by deception

4.25   The Theft Acts 1968 and 1978 create no fewer than seven offences of procuring various kinds of benefit by deception. They are:

1. Obtaining property.[70]
2. Obtaining a pecuniary advantage.[71]
3. Procuring the execution of a valuable security.[72]
4. Obtaining services.[73]
5. Securing the remission of a liability.[74]
6. Inducing a creditor to wait for or to forgo payment.[75]

> premises and facilities to make a secret profit, will that secret profit
> be subject to a constructive trust in favour of the employer?

The court's answer was:

> If, which we do not believe, it is properly described as a trust, it is
> not such a trust as falls within the ambit of section 5(1) of the
> Theft Act 1968.

And the court answered no to the third question—namely, whether, if its answer to the second question was yes, the constructive trust gave the employer a proprietary right or interest in the secret profit for the purpose of that subsection.

[69]   In WP 104 we expressed the provisional view that it would not: paras 10.50-10.52. The response on consultation was divided. Support for the view that the dishonest making of secret profits should be an offence was expressed by: Mr Justice Phillips; the Crown Prosecution Service; the Society of Public Teachers of Law; the Bar Council (in cases where the defendant had *actual* knowledge of the relevant prohibition); the Home Office; the Confederation of British Industry; and Mr G R Sullivan. Professor Sir John Smith favoured some regulation going beyond the civil law. Commentators who opposed that approach, on the ground that civil remedies were adequate, included the Metropolitan and City Police Company Fraud Department and British Telecom.

[70]   1968 Act, s 15.

[71]   1968 Act, s 16.

[72]   1968 Act, s 20(2).

[73]   1978 Act, s 1.

[74]   1978 Act, s 2(1)(a).

[75]   1978 Act, s 2(1)(b).

7. Obtaining an exemption from or abatement of liability.[76]

The relevant provisions of the Acts are set out in Appendix D to this report.

4.26   Unfortunately it seems that this array of offences may be inadequate to catch certain serious and prevalent frauds, namely those involving the obtaining of mortgage advances and other loans.[77]

4.27   These frauds, which constitute a major problem, are commonly charged as the obtaining of *property* by deception;[78] but whether this is appropriate will depend on how the advance is paid and what property is alleged to have been obtained. If the advance is paid by cheque, a charge of obtaining the cheque itself appears to be legally sound: the fact that the lender can recover the cheque from its bank after clearance does not negate the requisite intention permanently to deprive.[79]

4.28   If, however (as is increasingly common), the advance is paid by a direct transfer from the lender's bank account to that of the borrower, or the borrower's solicitor or other agent, no tangible property is obtained. If a charge of obtaining property by deception can be sustained at all it can only be in relation to the *intangible* property consisting in the credit balance obtained. But the offence requires that the property obtained by deception should belong to another, at least until the defendant obtains it. The credit to the borrower's account does not exist until the funds are transferred, and as soon as it comes into existence it belongs to the borrower himself. It *corresponds* to the property of which the lender is deprived when the equivalent sum is debited to the lender's account, but it is not the *same* property. In *Crick*[80] the Court of Appeal held that the offence can be committed in this situation, but this point does not appear to have been argued.

4.29   Another of the deception offences is tailor-made for the case where the defendant acquires *rights* rather than the victim's property, namely the offence of procuring the execution of a valuable security by deception.[81] But there are a number of ways in which funds can now be transferred from one account to another without the need for a cheque, and it is far from clear whether all of them involve the "execution" of a "valuable security" within the meaning of the Act. In *King*[82] it was held that a

---

[76]   1978 Act, s 2(1)(c).

[77]   See Professor Sir John Smith, "Mortgage frauds" [1993] 3 Archbold News p 6.

[78]   Theft Act 1968, s 15(1).

[79]   *Duru* [1974] 1 WLR 2.

[80]   *The Times*, 18 August 1993.

[81]   Theft Act 1968, s 20(2).

[82]   [1992] 1 QB 20.

CHAPS[83] order was a valuable security; but in *Manjdadria*[84] it was held that a telegraphic transfer was not, and *King* was described as a case "in which perhaps the extreme boundaries of a valuable security were canvassed". In any event the contention that a particular form of payment involves the execution of a valuable security must be supported by evidence of how it works.[85] Even if the problem is surmountable where the funds have actually been advanced, on a charge of *conspiracy* to procure the execution of a valuable security by deception it must be proved that the defendants *intended* to procure the execution of a valuable security;[86] and they may not have given the *means* of payment any thought.

4.30   A third possibility is the offence of obtaining *services* from another by deception.[87] Whether or not the provision of a mortgage advance or other loan is naturally described as a service is immaterial, since it is provided that:

> It is an obtaining of services where the other is induced to confer a benefit by doing some act, or causing or permitting some act to be done, on the understanding that the benefit has been or will be paid for.[88]

4.31   When a financial institution is induced to advance money by way of loan it confers a benefit for which it certainly expects to be paid (normally in the form of interest charges, an arrangement fee or both), and it would therefore seem that there is an obtaining of services within the meaning of the section. But in *Halai*[89] this was held not to be so. O'Connor LJ said, giving the judgment of the court:

> In our judgment, a mortgage advance cannot be described as a service. A mortgage advance is the lending of money for property and can

---

[83]   Clearing House Automated Payment System. The System is operated by a company owned by the major clearing banks. It can be used only for "irrevocable guaranteed unconditional sterling payment for same day settlement". A bank or customer who wishes to make payments through CHAPS makes its payments through its electronic terminal (a "gateway") to the recipient's gateway or, if the recipient member is not itself a CHAPS settlement member, the recipient's settlement bank. Settlement is effected by each settlement bank transmitting to the Bank of England's CHAPS gateway the details of its end-of-day net position with every other settlement bank. The Bank of England then makes the appropriate payments across the settlement banks' accounts with it. Because (so far as concerns CHAPS and its settlement banks) payment through CHAPS is unconditional, it is effectively immediate.

[84]   [1993] Crim LR 73.

[85]   *Bolton* (1992) 94 Cr App R 74.

[86]   *Dhillon* [1992] Crim LR 889.

[87]   Theft Act 1978, s 1(1).

[88]   Theft Act 1978, s 1(2).

[89]   [1983] Crim LR 624.

properly be charged under section 15 of the 1968 Act, if the facts support it. This count should never have been in the indictment.

We believe this to be wrong: the court appears to have applied the ordinary meaning of the word "services" rather than the extremely wide statutory definition. The decision has been heavily criticised,[90] and was said by Lord Lane CJ, giving the judgment of the Court of Appeal in *Teong Sun Chuah*,[91] to have "all the hallmarks of a decision *per incuriam*"; but in the absence of legislation, only the House of Lords can overrule it.

4.32   Clearly the substantive law of deception is failing adequately to meet the problem of loan fraud. Prosecutors are forced to fall back on conspiracy to defraud because it is the only charge which is unlikely to be defeated by purely technical arguments which have no relevance to the reality of the fraud alleged. This problem is of considerable practical significance. Moreover, unlike many of the problems which we canvass here, it is capable of resolution by means of a short and simple legislative provision.

4.33   *We accordingly recommend* that it should be made clear that the offence under section 1 of the Theft Act 1978, of dishonestly obtaining services by deception, extends to the dishonest obtaining by deception of loans of money.

8.   **The obtaining without deception of benefits other than property**

4.34   The Theft Acts draw a sharp distinction between property and other kinds of benefit. The dishonest acquisition of property may be an offence under section 15 of the Theft Act 1968 if it is done by deception, and may be theft if it is not (or,

---

[90] In a case-note on *Halai* in [1983] Crim LR 625, 626, Professor Sir John Smith expresses the following criticism (among others):

> [S]urely it is undeniable that when a building society is induced
> to make a mortgage advance it "is induced to confer a benefit by
> doing some act ... on the understanding that the benefit ... will
> be paid for". There is clearly an act, there is no doubt that it
> confers a benefit and it is certainly going to be paid for by the
> interest charged. In that case it is an obtaining of services
> within the section. Of course, as the court says, this could
> properly be charged as an offence of obtaining property by deception,
> contrary to section 15 of the 1968 Act. There is, however, nothing
> to suggest that the offences are mutually exclusive. Indeed, section
> 1 of the 1978 Act seems to overlap both section 15 and section 16(2)(b)
> [see Appendix D below] of the 1968 Act.

Professor Edward Griew describes the decision as "puzzling and regrettable" and points out that some loans may not involve obtaining "property", so that section 15 of the 1968 Act may not be available: *The Theft Acts 1968 and 1978* (6th ed 1990) para 8-08.

[91] [1991] Crim LR 463. The court consisted of Lord Lane CJ, Boreham and Judge JJ.

according to *Gomez*,[92] even if it is). In the case of other kinds of benefit there are a number of offences corresponding to section 15, and requiring that a benefit be obtained by deception; but there is no counterpart to theft. A person who dishonestly obtains a benefit other than property, otherwise than by deception, will not normally be guilty of an offence.[93]

4.35 However, experience has revealed cases where the need for a deception in the case of benefits other than property can cause difficulty. Perhaps the commonest example is the dishonest use of credit cards, cheque guarantee cards, and other instruments which confer on the person accepting them a right to payment from a bank or other financial institution. If a person dishonestly buys *goods* with the aid of a payment card which he is not authorised to use, the effect of *Gomez* is that he steals the goods (though that is scarcely an appropriate charge); whether he obtains them by deception is not so clear. Where he buys *services*, or any other benefit which cannot be categorised as property, the latter question becomes crucial.

4.36 It may be arguable in such a case that the benefit *is* obtained by deception. In *Charles*[94] the House of Lords held that a person who proffered a cheque guarantee card could be regarded as making an implied representation that he had the bank's authority to do so, and that if he knew otherwise then the benefit he thereby obtained could be regarded as having been obtained by deception. In *Lambie*[95] the House applied similar reasoning to the use of a credit card.

4.37 The difficulty is that the unauthorised use of a payment instrument cannot be *presumed* to be deceptive as a matter of law: the prosecution must adduce evidence that the person who was induced to accept the instrument was *in fact* deceived, and that it was as a *result* of that deception that the defendant obtained the benefit in question. Since the person accepting the instrument (or his employers) will usually in any event be entitled to claim payment from the issuing institution, whether or not the user is authorised to use it, the proposition that the user obtains the benefit by deceiving the acceptor is not without difficulty.

4.38 In *Charles* and *Lambie* the House of Lords explained this proposition by pointing out that the acceptor would presumably not accept the instrument by way of payment

---

[92] [1993] AC 442, in which the House of Lords held that the consent of the owner to the defendant's act, whether or not such consent was induced by deception, did not negative liability for theft.

[93] Specific offences (such as that of dishonestly abstracting electricity under the 1968 Act, s 13) apply to some kinds of benefit; and in other cases, eg, a pay-and-display (unmanned) car park, the offence of dishonestly making off without payment, contrary to s 3(1) of the 1978 Act (see para 4.52 below), may be available.

[94] [1977] AC 177.

[95] [1982] AC 449.

if he *knew* that the user had no authority to use it, because if he did so he would be a party to a fraud on the bank. This might impute to those who handle credit card transactions with fraudsters greater powers of analysis than in many cases they will possess. Unfortunately shop assistants, and others whose business it is to accept such payments, do not always perceive as clearly as lawyers the distinction between *not knowing whether* the customer has authority to use the instrument and *knowing that he does not,* and will often give evidence that they had no interest in his relationship with the bank and would still have accepted the payment in question had they known the truth. In the face of evidence to this effect a submission of no case ought to succeed.

4.39 The problem can often be resolved by resorting to other offences, even where the benefit obtained is not property and theft of the *benefit* is therefore not available. If the payment instrument belongs to someone other than the user then he will probably be guilty of stealing it, handling it[96] or both. If it is forged he will be guilty of one or more offences under the Forgery and Counterfeiting Act 1981. If he knows that the debit balance of the account relating to the payment instrument will be automatically cleared by a credit from an account in the name of another person, he may be guilty of stealing the credit balance of that account.[97] But it may be that an offence of deception is the only possible charge, and even that may be fraught with difficulty. The reality, usually, is that loss is being dishonestly inflicted on the bank. If this is done as part of a concerted scheme then it seems to us that the scheme can properly be charged as a conspiracy to defraud.

9.   Deception of computers and other machines

4.40 A further example of the obtaining of benefits other than property, without a "deception" within the meaning of the Theft Acts, is the case where it is only a computer or other machine that is (in a loose sense) deceived. The "deception" of a machine for the purpose of appropriating *property*[98] will normally found a charge of theft.[99] So, for example, if a credit balance in a bank account is appropriated by the making of false entries in the bank's computerised accounts, the fact that the entries involve a "deception" of the computer is merely incidental:

---

[96]   Theft Act 1968, s 22(1).

[97]   But he does not steal the funds used by the bank to meet the obligation he imposes on it: *Navvabi* [1986] 1 WLR 1311.

[98]   It was held to be larceny (and implicitly not obtaining by false pretences) to get cigarettes from a machine by using a brass disc instead of a coin: *Hands* (1887) 16 Cox CC 188.

[99]   As, now, will the deception of a person, since (except in the case of land) the offence of obtaining property by deception automatically constitutes theft: *Gomez* [1993] AC 442.

Appropriating property belonging to another is no less theft because it is done not by picking a pocket but by causing a computer to debit one account and to credit another.[100]

Where the benefit obtained is not property, however, different considerations apply. Although there is little direct authority on the matter,[101] it is generally accepted that for the purpose of offences of deception a human mind must be involved.[102] If the only victim of the "deception" is a machine, therefore, the deception offences will have no application.

4.41 There may be an offence none the less: some cases of dishonestly obtaining a benefit other than property are dealt with by specific statutory provision. There may be an offence of abstracting electricity,[103] as where a person inserts a metal disc instead of a coin into a machine in a launderette. It is an offence dishonestly to obtain a telecommunication service with intent to avoid payment of any charge applicable to it,[104] or to operate a parking meter otherwise than in the prescribed manner.[105] More generally, the offence of dishonestly making off without payment[106] "for any goods

---

[100] Smith and Hogan, *Criminal Law* (7th ed 1992) p 714.

[101] In *Clayman* (*The Times*, 1 July 1972) a trial judge ruled that it was not deception to jam a parking-meter with a ring from a beer-can. In *Davies v Flackett* [1973] RTR 8 (DC) the defendant parked his car in an unattended car park, the charge for use being 5p, which he intended to pay on leaving by placing a coin in a machine that raised a barrier on the exit route; on driving to the exit he found a stranger holding up the barrier, and he drove away without paying. The defendant was held not to have committed an offence under s 16 of the Theft Act 1968, of dishonestly obtaining by deception a pecuniary advantage, since he had obtained nothing *by* deception. Bridge J expressly doubted, obiter, whether in any event a deception could be practised without a human mind to be deceived (though Ackner J made it clear that he did not suggest that an offence could not be committed when there was some mishandling of a machine). See also *Moritz* (1981), unreported; para 4.43 below.

[102] "The whole law of deception is geared to the deception of humans, and it would radically alter the concept if the courts extended it to the 'deception' of machinery or electronic gadgets. Happily, the courts have not so far shown a disposition to take this step": Glanville Williams, *Textbook of Criminal Law* (2nd ed 1983) p 794.

[103] 1968 Act, s 13, which consists in dishonestly using electricity without due authority, or dishonestly causing it to be wasted or diverted. The offence is triable either way: Magistrates' Courts Act 1980, s 17, Sch 1, para 28. The maximum punishment on conviction on indictment is 5 years' imprisonment.

[104] Telecommunications Act 1984, s 42. The offence is triable either way. The maximum punishment for conviction on indictment is an unlimited fine and 2 years' imprisonment.

[105] Road Traffic Regulation Act 1984, s 35A(2) (added by the Parking Act 1989, s 2, replacing previous legislation).

[106] Introduced by the Theft Act 1978, s 3. The maximum penalty for the offence, which is triable either way, is 2 years' imprisonment: s 4(2)(b).

supplied or service done" extends to cases in which the evasion of payment includes, or takes the form of, deceiving a machine.[107]

4.42 Offences under the Computer Misuse Act 1990, though not aimed specifically at the *deception* of a computer, may indirectly cover some cases. The Act, which implemented our recommendations,[108] creates three offences. Two relate essentially to conduct preparatory to the commission primarily (though not exclusively) of offences of dishonesty. They concern "hacking", the unauthorised accessing of computer material. Of those two offences, one is the basic offence;[109] the other is an "aggravated" offence, requiring the ulterior intent of committing or facilitating the commission of an arrestable offence.[110] The third offence deals with the unauthorised modification of computer material (for example, by a fraudulent bank employee who causes a computer to debit one person's account and credit his own).

4.43 The dishonest deception of a machine has been specifically addressed by legislation in relation to VAT and to forgery. As to VAT, in *Moritz*[111] a trial judge held that, given the computer-assisted nature of the processing of VAT returns, there was no satisfactory evidence that in submitting an admittedly false VAT return the defendant had intended to "deceive" in the required sense. However, the judge apparently assumed that the defendant *knew* that no person was going to act on the false statements.[112] Moreover, in cases like *Moritz* the defendant may be guilty of theft:

> If a tradesman makes a dishonest claim on the appropriate form for the repayment of VAT input tax and the claim, without being read by anyone, is fed into a computer which automatically produces a cheque

---

[107] eg to facts such as those of *Davies v Flackett* (para 4.40, n 101 above). The term "service" is not defined in the section; but the facility of parking in an unmanned car-park would seem to be within its scope. Another example might arise under s 5(3) of the Regulation of Railways Act 1889. Under that provision it is a summary offence if a person, with intent to avoid payment of his fare, (i) travels or attempts to travel on a railway without previously paying the fare or (ii) "having paid his fare for a certain distance, knowingly and wilfully proceeds by train beyond that distance without previously paying the additional fare for the additional distance". One method of committing the offence would be to use, say, a bogus or stolen card to trigger the mechanism of an automatic barrier. Such conduct may also constitute the offence of making off without payment: *Moberly v Allsop* (1992) 156 JP 514 (DC) (in which a traveller on the London Underground was held to be still "on the spot" when going through the exit barrier at his destination).

[108] Criminal Law: Computer Misuse (1989) Law Com No 186, Cm 819.

[109] Under s 1 (set out in Appendix D hereto), of causing a computer to perform a function with intent to secure unauthorised access.

[110] Section 2. The offence, triable only on indictment, carries a maximum punishment of 5 years' imprisonment.

[111] (1981), unreported. See the Report of the Keith Committee on Enforcement Powers of the Revenue Departments (1983) Cmnd 8822, vol 2, para 18.3.17.

[112] Professor Sir John Smith, *The Law of Theft* (7th ed 1993) para 4-09.

for the sum claimed, this may be regarded as indistinguishable from obtaining the cigarettes by the foreign coin [as in *Hands*; see paragraph 4.40, footnote 98 above]. The clerks who feed the document into the machine and put the cheque in the envelope are innocent agents—like an eight-year-old child, told to put the foreign coin in the machine and bring home the cigarettes.[113]

The VAT legislation now provides that an intent to deceive extends to an "intent to secure that a machine will respond to [a] document as if it were a true document".[114]

4.44   The intended deception of a machine is also addressed in the Forgery and Counterfeiting Act 1981. Sections 1 and 3 of the Act provide for twin offences. One offence, under section 1, is of *making* a "false instrument"; the other, under section 3, of *using* such an instrument, with the intention (in either case) that the defendant or another person "shall use it to induce somebody to accept it as genuine, and by reason of so accepting it to do or not to do some act to his own or any other person's prejudice". Section 10(3) and (4) provides:

> (3)   In this Part of this Act references to inducing somebody to accept a false instrument as genuine ... include references to inducing a machine to respond to the instrument ... as if it were a genuine instrument ... .

> (4)   Where subsection (3) above applies, the act or omission intended to be induced by the machine responding to the instrument ... shall be treated as an act or omission to a person's prejudice.

These subsections would apply, for example, to making a false bank card for the purpose of obtaining an automated pay-out.[115] Another case might be the forging of a pass for the purpose of gaining access to (say) a building by using it in a machine programmed to respond to authorised passes.[116]

---

[113] *Ibid* (footnote omitted). As Professor Smith points out, this conduct also amounts to forgery under the Forgery and Counterfeiting Act 1981, s 10(3), considered at para 4.44 below.

[114] Value Added Tax Act 1983, s 39(2C), introduced by s 12(5) of the Finance Act 1985. The new subsection implemented a recommendation in the Report of the Keith Committee (see para 4.43, n 111 above), vol 2, para 18.4.2, to meet the ruling in *Moritz*.

[115] If the defendant obtains payment, he is guilty of theft: see para 4.40 above.

[116] "Prejudice" is not restricted to economic prejudice: under s 10(1)(c), it includes the result of a person's acceptance of a false instrument as genuine in connection with his performance of a duty. The machine is regarded, in effect, as being under a duty.

4.45   In 1993 we conducted detailed consultations with a range of business organisations under the aegis of the Confederation of British Industry, including the British Bankers' Association, British Telecom and the Association of British Insurers; and with the Credit Industry Fraud Avoidance System. The sole purpose of our consultations was to elicit whether in practice there were, or were likely to be developed in the near future, any systems involving the supply of false information to a machine which warranted the creation of a new, specific sanction because no human mind was concerned in the "decision" made by the machine. The organisations consulted were unable, in some cases after discussion, to identify any such procedure.[117]

4.46   It is of course conceivable that this interim view may be incorrect or that the rapid pace of technological change may render it necessary to consider at a future date the introduction of a new offence or offences relating to the deception of a machine. We have concluded that for practical purposes there is at present no significant or clearly established lacuna in that respect in the existing scheme of substantive dishonesty offences. However, this question, among many others, will fall for consideration in our forthcoming review of dishonesty offences. It would clearly be inappropriate to consider the matter in isolation, outside the context of that review; and it is most unlikely that this, or any other issue arising from the present scheme of dishonesty offences, will receive legislative attention pending our review.

10.   Evasion of liability without intent to make permanent default

4.47   Under section 16(2)(a) of the Theft Act 1968 a person who dishonestly and by deception induced his creditor to wait for payment of a debt was held to be guilty of an offence.[118] When that paragraph was replaced by the provisions of the Theft Act 1978 Parliament accepted the recommendation of the CLRC[119] that such conduct should not be an offence unless the defendant's intention is to make permanent default, in whole or in part. An agreement dishonestly to deceive creditors into waiting for payment is therefore not a conspiracy to evade liability by deception unless it is intended that the debts shall never be paid;[120] but this should be a conspiracy to defraud in any event, since it is an agreement to deprive the creditors (albeit temporarily) of the money to which they are entitled.

---

[117]   Subsequently (and separately), we consulted the Association for Payment Clearing Services. That organisation suggests that no substantive offence may be committed by a fraudulent retailer who sends details of fictitious transactions to the bank (his "acquirer") which handles his credit card transactions, knowing that his account will be credited automatically and without the intervention of a human mind. It is not clear that such conduct is covered by the offence of forgery or by an offence of computer misuse.

[118]   *Turner* [1974] AC 357.

[119]   Criminal Law Revision Committee, Thirteenth Report, Section 16 of the Theft Act 1968 (1977), Cmnd 6733, para 6.

[120]   Theft Act 1978, s 2(1)(b).

4.48   In *Zemmel* the Court of Appeal declined to accept that, the 1978 Act notwithstanding,

> by a side wind the common law has suddenly re-emerged to reinstate or create as a crime that which Parliament thought it right to take off the statute book as a crime.[121]

But it is clear that the temporary appropriation of property belonging to another can ground a charge of conspiracy to defraud although Parliament decided in 1968 that it should not amount to theft.[122] It seems difficult to understand why, if the common law survives in that case, it should have been impliedly abrogated in this.

4.49   The CLRC thought that the debtor whose deception is intended merely to buy more time does not deserve prosecution, and in the ordinary case this is doubtless true. But the Serious Fraud Office has told us of more than one case where the defendants painted a false picture of their affairs so as to dissuade creditors from calling in the money owed to them. The defendants did not intend never to pay, but only to subject their creditors to a *risk* of non-payment which they would not have accepted had they known the truth. In these cases it was possible to charge fraudulent trading;[123] but had the fraudulent business not been a company incorporated in Great Britain, it would have been necessary to fall back on conspiracy to defraud (presumably in the hope of distinguishing *Zemmel*). We believe that it should be possible to prosecute for such conduct, whether or not a company is involved.

11.   A false general impression

4.50   In WP 104[124] we drew attention to cases where, though the facts alleged probably amount in theory to an obtaining by deception, it is in practice difficult for the prosecution to establish exactly what false representations were made, or from what conduct they can be implied. This is most commonly so where the defendants have

---

[121]   (1985) 81 Cr App R 279, 284.

[122]   See para 4.10 above.

[123]   Companies Act 1985, s 458. In *Re Murray-Watson Ltd*, 6 April 1977, unreported, Oliver J stated that the section was aimed at the carrying on of a business, not at "the execution of individual transactions in the course of" that activity. Subsequently, however, in *Re Gerald Cooper Chemicals Ltd* [1978] Ch 262, 268, Templeman J stated that a single transaction could suffice, provided that the transaction could be described as a fraud on a creditor perpetrated in the course of carrying on a business; and in *Re Sarflax Ltd* [1979] Ch 592, 598F-G, Oliver J accepted that his observations in *Re Murray-Watson Ltd* might require some qualification in the light of the views expressed by Templeman J. More recently, in *Lockwood* [1986] Crim LR 244, the Court of Appeal dismissed an appeal against a conviction under s 458, in which one ground of appeal was that a single transaction sufficed "only in special circumstances"; but the court apparently did not consider this point.

[124]   At paras 4.15-4.19.

been carrying on what purports to be a legitimate business but it is alleged that their intention was to defraud those doing business with them.

4.51 An example is the "long firm fraud", where the defendants, ostensibly as an ordinary trading concern, obtain goods on credit for which they have no intention of paying. If the fraudulent business is incorporated then it may be convenient to charge the offence of fraudulent trading;[125] otherwise (assuming that more than one person can be proved to have been dishonestly involved) the prosecution is likely to charge conspiracy to defraud, in the hope of avoiding the pitfalls of the law of deception. We understand that prosecutors would face significantly greater difficulties in this kind of case if conspiracy to defraud were not available. However, we do not think this is properly categorised as a potential gap in the law: rather, it is an example of the kind of practical consideration that we discuss in Part V below.

12. Dishonest failure to pay for goods or services

4.52 Section 3(1) of the Theft Act 1978 provides for an offence of dishonestly making off without payment.[126] In *Allen*[127] the House of Lords held that a person does not have the necessary "intent to avoid payment of the amount due" unless he intends *never* to pay. If his intention is merely to *delay* payment then, however dishonest he may be, he commits no offence. Where, however, two or more people agree dishonestly to make off without payment, intending eventually to pay in full, it would seem that they would be guilty of a conspiracy to defraud. Their intention is dishonestly to cause prejudice by depriving their creditor of the sum due between the time when they ought to pay and the time when they intend to pay. This appears to be a potential gap in the law, albeit hardly a serious one.

13. Gambling swindles

4.53 There are certain kinds of gambling swindle which appear to fall outside the law of theft and deception. In WP 104 we gave the following example:

> If A lays a bet with B that C's horse will win a race and, later, to make this more likely, A drugs the other horses in the race, with the result that C's horse does win and B pays A a sum of money, there is neither an appropriation nor an operative deception. It is, however, arguable that A's behaviour is dishonest and deserving of criminal sanction and that if A acted following an agreement with another the conduct would be within the scope of conspiracy to defraud.[128]

---

[125] Companies Act 1985, s 458.

[126] See Appendix D below.

[127] [1985] AC 1029.

[128] WP 104, para 4.30.

It may now be arguable that A is stealing the winnings from B: it is no defence that B consented to pay.[129] It might even be arguable that A obtains the money from B by deception, namely a false representation that C's horse has won the race fairly, or at least that A does not know otherwise. But few prosecutors would confidently rely on either charge.

4.54 By section 17 of the Gaming Act 1845 it is an offence to employ a "fraud or unlawful device or ill practice" in connection with gaming or wagering;[130] but it appears that the "fraud or unlawful device or ill practice" must be employed during the playing of the game.[131] Nor would these swindles necessarily fall within section 16(2)(c) of the Theft Act 1968, by virtue of which a person may be guilty of obtaining a pecuniary advantage by deception[132] if as a result of his deception he is given the opportunity to win money by betting. The fraud may involve no deception at all.

4.55 In our view, and that of respondents who addressed the point, this kind of conduct ought to be criminal; and it appears that in some cases it is only the existence of conspiracy to defraud that makes it so. In the course of our review of the law of dishonesty we hope to advance proposals for the amendment or replacement of section 17 of the Gaming Act: we discussed some possible ways of doing this in Appendix B to WP 104. In the meantime we regard this as a potential gap in the law which needs to be filled, and which is at present partially filled by conspiracy to defraud.

14. Corruption not involving consideration

4.56 We were informed by a number of prosecutors of cases in which employees have acted to their employers' detriment but in which it cannot be established that the employees have received any benefit. In such cases, it is often difficult or impossible to prove the offer or payment of an inducement, which is necessary for the purpose of a corruption charge.[133] But they are *defrauding* their employers whether they receive an inducement or not. The Serious Fraud Office informed us of one case, for example, in which it was alleged that an employee of a local authority had concealed the fact that the authority was not receiving from a contractor the level of service to which it was entitled. In our view, the question whether or not the employee received payment for his conduct is immaterial to the question whether the authority was defrauded.

---

[129] *Gomez* [1993] AC 442.

[130] The section is set out in Appendix D below.

[131] *Lawler* (1850) 14 JP 561; *R v Governor of Brixton Prison, ex p Sjoland* [1912] 3 KB 568; *Moore* (1914) 10 Cr App R 54.

[132] Theft Act 1968, s 16(1). Section 16 is set out in Appendix D below.

[133] Public Bodies Corrupt Practices Act 1889, s 1; Prevention of Corruption Act 1906, s 1(1).

4.57 Similarly we are told that it is increasingly common for those desiring confidential information, for example the details of bids submitted by competitors for a contract, to pay agents to acquire it. The principal in such an arrangement (like the prosecution) may have no idea whether the information is obtained by bribery, deception or otherwise; but he will at least know that the process of getting it is bound to involve dishonesty of one kind or another, because the information is of such a character that it cannot legitimately be obtained at all. He is therefore party to a conspiracy to defraud. Indeed one respondent pointed out that in this situation one of the main objections to conspiracy to defraud, namely that it catches conduct which is not criminal on the part of an individual, does not apply: collusion is the essence of the matter.

15. "Prejudice" without financial loss[134]

4.58 In WP 104 we referred to

> the case where the dishonesty is not aimed at securing any financial advantage and in consequence there is no possibility of financial prejudice to another, whether or not he is the person upon whom the dishonesty is practised.[135]

We referred to cases of this kind as "non-economic frauds"; but, although no economic *loss* may be intended, those who practise fraud of any kind nearly always act with a view to economic *gain* for themselves. The distinction between these cases and more conventional frauds is that the "prejudice" which the fraudster seeks to cause is prejudice of a non-economic kind—namely the inducing of the person prejudiced to do something he would not otherwise have done (or to refrain from doing that which he would otherwise have done)—and that the intended gain is intended to follow only indirectly from that prejudice.

4.59 The possibility that such conduct might constitute fraud was confirmed by the House of Lords in *Welham*,[136] where forged documents had been used for the purpose of evading statutory credit restrictions. It was held that the necessary intent to defraud had been established because the appellant had intended to deceive those responsible for enforcing the legislation into failing to do so. In *Withers*[137] the House confirmed that the same principle was applicable to conspiracy to defraud. In *Scott*[138] Lord Diplock suggested that it applied only where the victim was "a person

---

[134] We outlined the present law at paras 2.6-2.8 above, under the heading "Non-economic loss".

[135] WP 104, para 4.45.

[136] [1961] AC 103.

[137] [1975] AC 842, for the facts of which see para 2.8, n 18 above.

[138] [1975] AC 819.

performing public duties" and not where he was "a private individual".[139]

4.60 In WP 104 we examined several kinds of conduct potentially falling within the *Welham* principle, and concluded that if the principle applied only to persons performing public duties then it caught very little conduct that was caught by no other offence.[140] We further expressed the provisional view that if conspiracy to defraud were abolished it would be neither necessary nor desirable to fill the resulting gap by creating an offence of inducing a person performing a public duty to act contrary to that duty.[141] This was partly because we were not aware of any cases where conspiracy to defraud had been charged in such circumstances, and partly because it would be too difficult to provide a satisfactory definition of the concept of a public duty. We were therefore willing to contemplate with comparative equanimity the prospect of such conduct ceasing to be criminal altogether.

4.61 Neither of these reasons now appears to us as convincing as it then did. In the first place we now know that conspiracy to defraud *is* occasionally useful in such cases. An example is *Moses*,[142] where immigration officials were deceived into issuing national insurance numbers.

4.62 Secondly, our assumption in the Working Paper that the *Welham* principle applies only to public duties now appears to have been unfounded. Lord Diplock's attempt to restrict the principle in this way was rejected by the Privy Council in *Wai Yu-tsang*:

> ... the cases concerned with persons performing public duties are not to be regarded as a special category in the manner described by Lord Diplock, but rather as exemplifying the general principle that conspiracies to defraud are not restricted to cases of intention to cause the victim economic loss.[143]

If this is an accurate statement of English law then the offence would extend to an agreement dishonestly to induce an employee of a private concern (such as a

---

[139] [1975] AC 819, 841.

[140] WP 104, paras 4.51-4.58.

[141] *Ibid*, paras 10.56-10.60.

[142] [1991] Crim LR 617; see para 2.7 above. As Professor Sir John Smith points out in a commentary on the case, the obtaining by the immigrants of the plastic card bearing a national insurance number may have constituted the offence of obtaining property by deception, contrary to s 15 of the Theft Act 1968; but "the gist of the offence was the allocation of the number—it was not, in substance, a property offence and it would have been inappropriate to charge a conspiracy to commit an offence under section 15".

[143] [1992] 1 AC 269, 277F *per* Lord Goff of Chieveley, delivering the advice of the Judicial Committee.

bank)[144] to provide confidential information on its customers' affairs. Such conduct might not have the effect of inflicting economic loss on the victim in all cases, unlike the dishonest acquisition of its trade secrets;[145] but it should arguably be criminal none the less.

16. Assisting in fraud by third parties

4.63   In *Hollinshead*[146] the defendants had agreed to make and sell devices (known as "black boxes") whose only function was to affect the proper functioning of electricity meters and thus conceal the amount of electricity actually used. The Court of Appeal held that this was neither a conspiracy to defraud nor a statutory conspiracy, because the contemplated fraud was to be committed by persons who were strangers to the agreement. The House of Lords held that it was a conspiracy to defraud, because its sole purpose was dishonest.[147]

4.64   It is not clear whether such conduct amounts *only* to conspiracy to defraud, because it is not clear that it is not a conspiracy to aid and abet the substantive offence committed by the third party. Under section 1(1) of the Criminal Law Act 1977 a person is guilty of conspiracy if he

> agrees with any other person or persons that a course of conduct shall be pursued which will necessarily amount to or involve the commission of any offence or offences by one or more of the parties to the agreement if the agreement is carried out in accordance with their intentions ... .

4.65   In *Hollinshead* the Court of Appeal held that the agreement fell outside this provision because the use of the devices would not have involved the commission of an offence "by one or more of the parties to the agreement" within the meaning of the Act, although the parties to the agreement would clearly have been guilty of aiding and abetting the offence committed by the user. The House of Lords did not think it necessary to express a view, but Lord Roskill suggested that

> in any future case in which that question does arise it should be treated as open for consideration de novo, as much may depend on the particular facts of the case in question.[148]

---

[144] Cf *Withers*, para 2.8, n 18 above.

[145] Cf para 4.7 above.

[146] [1985] AC 975.

[147] In *James* (1985) 82 Cr App R 226, on similar facts, the Court of Appeal said that a count of conspiracy to defraud would "without question" have fitted the facts.

[148] [1985] AC 975, 998E.

Thus it is not clear how much weight can be given to the decision of the Court of Appeal on this point.[149] But if that decision was right, and an agreement to assist in an offence of dishonesty by a third party is not a statutory conspiracy, it follows that such an agreement is criminal *only* by virtue of being (as the House of Lords held) a conspiracy to defraud.[150]

4.66   The CLRC welcomed the House of Lords' decision in *Hollinshead*.[151] We express no view on the question whether the defendants' conduct in that case was rightly regarded as amounting to a conspiracy to defraud, but we agree that such conduct ought to be criminal. None of our respondents suggested otherwise.[152] In our recent consultation paper on Assisting and Encouraging Crime[153] we provisionally proposed the creation of a new offence of assisting crime, which, broadly speaking, would be committed by anyone who knowingly provides assistance in the commission of an offence by another. The offence would be inchoate in character, in the sense that it would be committed whether or not the person expected to commit the offence as a principal offender actually did so. We also proposed that the new offence should be subject to the ordinary law of conspiracy, so that an agreement to assist crime would be a conspiracy to commit that offence. At the present time we have not decided on the policy that we will adopt in our final report on Assisting and Encouraging Crime.

[149]   Professor J C Smith suggests that if there can be a statutory conspiracy to aid and abet, *Hollinshead* was necessarily wrongly decided by the House of Lords; but that, it being a decision of the House of Lords, it must be presumed that it is right and that an indictment will not lie under s 1 of the Criminal Law Act 1977 for conspiring to aid and abet: see [1985] Crim LR 655, 656.

[150]   Smith and Hogan, *Criminal Law* (7th ed 1992) p 280.

[151]   Criminal Law Revision Committee, Eighteenth Report: Conspiracy to Defraud (1986) Cmnd 9873, para 3.14. The Committee did not, however, elaborate. Cf J R Spencer, [1985] CLJ 336, 339:

>   [T]he House of Lords have been very naughty to bend the definition of conspiracy like this. It is hard to be too cross, however, because only by doing this could they ensure that certain people who unquestionably deserve punishment do not go free. At the back of [this decision] there lies the fact that there is no general offence ... of deliberately facilitating another person to commit a crime, and hence no obvious offence for the man who provides a criminal with his equipment. ... The result is not satisfactory, however, because the cost of catching facilitators in this way is much artificiality, and an offence of conspiracy which is dangerously wide in other respects.

[152]   Few of those who responded to WP 104 commented on this matter. There was, however, a measure of support for a further study of "facilitation" as a general offence. In particular, the Metropolitan and City Police Company Fraud Department and (we were informed by the Association of Chief Police Officers) the Metropolitan Police Specialist Operations thought that such an offence would be of considerable assistance in dealing with crime generally. There was, by contrast, no support for the alternative approach of creating an offence of conspiracy to aid and abet.

[153]   (1993) Law Commission Consultation Paper No 131.

4.67 If the law were changed in accordance with these provisional proposals, an agreement such as that in *Hollinshead* would fall within section 1(1) of the Criminal Law Act 1977, and it would be unnecessary to rely upon conspiracy to defraud. If conspiracy to defraud were abolished *without* any such change, however, the effect would probably be that such an agreement would cease to be criminal. We would regard such an outcome as unfortunate. As we pointed out in that consultation paper, the fact that the present law formally prevents a conviction in respect of any form of aiding crime gives rise to concern: "people who provide devices ... to abstract electricity can be argued to merit control and punishment ... irrespective of whether the persons supplied actually go on and commit the offences envisaged by their suppliers".[154]

4.68 Since we have not yet considered whether our final recommendations on assisting and encouraging crime should follow our provisional proposals, and we do not know whether or when, if they do, the recommendations are likely to be implemented, we regard this as an argument for the retention of conspiracy to defraud for the time being.

17. Ignorance of the details of the fraud

4.69 We have been informed by a number of prosecutors of cases in which it is clear that substantive offences have been committed in the furtherance of a fraudulent scheme, but it is doubtful whether persons on the fringe of the scheme can be charged as parties to those offences, or to conspiracies to commit them, because there is insufficient evidence that they knew the details of what was planned. In a mortgage fraud, for example, if a number of defendants are charged with a substantive offence of deception, or with conspiracy to commit such an offence, the prosecution must prove that each defendant knew what form the deception was to take and how the desired benefit was to be obtained—for example, in the case of a conspiracy to procure the execution of valuable securities by deception, *what* valuable securities were to be procured. It would not be sufficient to prove, against a particular defendant, that he knew in general terms that something dishonest was going on but was not sure of the details.

4.70 On a charge of conspiracy to defraud, however, this would be enough: fraud requires only the dishonest causing of prejudice, and one can therefore be a party to it without any detailed knowledge of how the prejudice is to be caused. In the Australian case of *Aston*[155] it was argued that a person is not party to a conspiracy to defraud unless he knows at least the "bare essentials" of the scheme—for example, that fictitious documents are to be used. The argument was rejected by the South Australian Court of Criminal Appeal:

---

[154] (1993) Law Commission Consultation Paper No 131, paras 3.18-3.19.

[155] (1987) 44 SASR 436.

This cannot possibly be the case; a person can be a willing conspirator in a fraudulent scheme, well knowing that the scheme is fraudulent, but having no idea of the manner in which it is implemented—not knowing any of the essential steps leading up to its implementation. If a person knows that a scheme is fraudulent and, nevertheless, participates in it, then he is as much guilty of the conspiracy to defraud as is the mastermind of the scheme.[156]

Thus, it is said, the effect of conspiracy to defraud can be to impose liability on a defendant who has knowingly participated in a fraud but might otherwise be guilty of no offence.

4.71 We are not convinced that prosecutors' pessimism as to the prospects of securing convictions of substantive offences against such defendants is entirely well founded. A person who has knowingly provided assistance towards the commission of an offence may be convicted of aiding and abetting the offence without proof that he knew *exactly* what offence was to be committed: it is sufficient that he knew the *type* of offence contemplated.[157] It would also be sufficient if he knew that the principal offender might commit one of several offences, and the principal did in fact do so.[158] These principles might in some cases catch the "fringe conspirator".

4.72 However, the regularity with which this point was made to us by very experienced prosecutors leads us to suspect that liability for aiding and abetting offences of dishonesty may not be as easy to establish in practice as the authorities might suggest. We believe that liability should extend, and should be clearly understood to extend, to a person who knowingly participates in a fraud without knowing exactly what substantive offences are to be committed, or how, or against whom. We regard this position as being broadly consistent with our provisional proposal in our recent consultation paper on Assisting and Encouraging Crime,[159] that it should be sufficient for the proposed new offence of assisting crime if the defendant knows or believes that his conduct will assist in the commission of one of a number of

---

[156] (1987) 44 SASR 436, 439, *per* O'Loughlin J.

[157] *Bainbridge* [1960] 1 QB 129.

[158] *Maxwell v DPP for Northern Ireland* [1978] 1 WLR 1350.

[159] (1993) Law Commission Consultation Paper No 131.

specific crimes, though he does not know which.[160] This appears to be the position in conspiracy to defraud, and we regard it as a desirable feature of the offence.

18. Commercial swindles

4.73 In WP 56[161] we examined under this heading a number of commercial swindles for which conspiracy to defraud appeared to be the most appropriate charge.[162] In WP 104, however,[163] we re-examined these cases and concluded that they could probably all have been charged as some other offence. Conspiracy to defraud might be the most *suitable* offence, for reasons discussed in Part V below, but it would not be the *only* offence. Therefore we do not regard these cases as potential gaps in the law.

C. SUMMARY

1. Conspiracy to defraud

4.74 Pending our review of the law of dishonesty, we conclude that conspiracy to defraud adds substantially to the reach of the criminal law in the case of the following kinds of conduct (or planned conduct) that in our view should, at least in certain circumstances, be criminal:

Conduct which would amount to "theft" if the property in question were capable of being stolen.[164]

Some cases in which the owner of property is temporarily deprived of it.[165]

Cases in which there is, for the purpose of the Theft Act 1968, no "property belonging to another".[166]

Secret profits made by employees and fiduciaries.[167]

---

[160] *Ibid*, para 4.88. We explained, at para 4.58:

> Where the principal crime is in the future, it would in our view be unreasonably restrictive to require knowledge or belief on the part of [the defendant] in all the detail that would be necessary in order to indict the principal crime. In particular, it should not be required that [the defendant] can necessarily state the time or place of the principal crime, or identify its victim.

[161] See para 1.4 above.

[162] WP 56, paras 42-47.

[163] WP 104, paras 4.20-4.29.

[164] Namely, land, things growing wild on land, and game; para 4.6 above.

[165] See paras 4.10-4.16 above.

[166] See paras 4.17-4.19 above.

[167] See paras 4.20-4.24 above.

The obtaining without deception of benefits other than property.[168]

The evasion of liability without intent to make permanent default.[169]

Dishonest failure to pay for goods or services.[170]

Gambling swindles.[171]

Corruption not involving consideration.[172]

"Prejudice" without financial loss.[173]

Assisting in fraud by third parties.[174]

Cases in which a party is ignorant of the *details* of the fraud.[175]

4.75   Conspiracy to defraud is also relevant to the criminal law relating to the unauthorised collection or disclosure of confidential information,[176] and to the unsanctioned temporary deprivation of property *in general*.[177] We express no opinion at this stage on whether it is right that this should be so.

2.   Obtaining loans of money by deception

4.76   *We recommend* **that it should be made clear that the offence under section 1 of the Theft Act 1978, of dishonestly obtaining services by deception, extends to the lending of money.**[178] We make this recommendation because we believe that a number of people who should be convicted of obtaining loans of money by deception are not being prosecuted at the present time.

---

[168] See paras 4.34-4.39 above.

[169] See paras 4.47-4.49 above.

[170] See para 4.52 above.

[171] See paras 4.53-4.55 above.

[172] See paras 4.56-4.57 above.

[173] See paras 4.58-4.62 above.

[174] See paras 4.63-4.68 above.

[175] See paras 4.69-4.72 above.

[176] See paras 4.7-4.9 above.

[177] See paras 4.10-4.16 above.

[178] See para 4.33 above.

PART V
PRACTICAL CONSIDERATIONS

A. GENERAL

5.1 The prosecutors whom we have consulted, while drawing our attention to the potential of conspiracy to defraud for filling gaps in the law, put greater emphasis on its *practical* advantages in cases of serious fraud. In some instances what was described to us as a practical advantage proved on closer examination to be a case where without conspiracy to defraud there might be no offence at all—such as the fringe conspirator who has insufficient knowledge to be charged with a substantive offence or with conspiracy to commit one[1]—but for the most part it was argued that conspiracy to defraud was often the most *appropriate* charge rather than the *only* one. Some of the alleged "advantages" of the offence, though undoubtedly advantages from the prosecutor's point of view (in the sense of making a case easier to prosecute and convictions easier to secure), could scarcely be regarded as desirable features of the offence in an objective sense: for example, the reduced likelihood of separate trials being ordered, or the avoidance of a requirement that the Director of Public Prosecutions[2] or the Attorney-General should consent to a charge of statutory conspiracy.[3] However, the main arguments advanced for retaining conspiracy to defraud on practical grounds appear to us to be compelling: they represent advantages not just for prosecutors but for the effective administration of justice.

5.2 In this context we have an advantage which is rarely available to us in considering whether a particular offence should continue to exist: namely a trial period during which, for most practical purposes, it did not. Between the decision of the House of Lords in *Ayres*[4] and the coming into force of section 12 of the Criminal Justice Act 1987, conspiracy to defraud could not be charged unless what was alleged did not amount to a conspiracy to commit any substantive offence.[5] During that period, its role was essentially confined to that of supplementing the substantive law. Conspiracies which would previously have been charged as conspiracy to defraud had to be charged as statutory conspiracies to commit substantive

---

[1] See paras 4.69-4.72 above.

[2] Under the Prosecution of Offences Act 1985, s 1(7), the consent of the Director of Public Prosecutions may now be given on her behalf by a Crown Prosecutor. The level of the Crown Prosecution Service at which the granting of consent to a prosecution is considered is a matter for administrative arrangements within the Service. A requirement of consent still has the effect that the propriety or otherwise of a prosecution must be considered *before* proceedings are commenced, "whereas in the normal case the CPS merely exercises a retrospective control, approving or disapproving a basic decision which has already been taken by the police": *Blackstone's Criminal Practice* (1994) para D1.79.

[3] Criminal Law Act 1977, s 4.

[4] [1984] AC 447.

[5] See paras 1.8-1.11 above.

offences—however inappropriate such a charge might be. The inconvenience ensuing from this rule was vividly described by the CLRC,[6] and Parliament was persuaded to reverse it. We regard this period as a salutary lesson on the dangers of removing from the prosecutor's armoury one of the main weapons against serious fraud.

B.   THE OVERALL CRIMINALITY

5.3   Perhaps the reason most often advanced by prosecutors for charging conspiracy to defraud, rather than a substantive offence or a statutory conspiracy, is that conspiracy to defraud paints a better picture of the overall fraud. This may be because the substantive offences committed in the course of a fraud are merely incidental to it,[7] or because their victim is someone other than the main victim of the fraud.[8] Alternatively the alleged fraud may consist of several limbs, most or all of which involve distinct substantive offences, but none of which can be singled out as the essence of the fraud. For example, the defendants may have defrauded both their bank and their trade creditors; or there may have been both a dishonest obtaining of money and a subsequent cover-up. In such circumstances many prosecutors will either charge the substantive offences (or statutory conspiracies to commit them) in separate counts, with a separate count of conspiracy to defraud, or rely on conspiracy to defraud alone. In either case the function of the charge of conspiracy to defraud is, it is said, to represent the "overall criminality".

5.4   This function appears to us to have at least two distinct aspects. In the first place it assists the prosecution in explaining to the jury how all the alleged incidents of dishonesty were part and parcel of an overall fraudulent scheme. This is in our view a clearly desirable objective.

5.5   Secondly, however, a charge of conspiracy to defraud also enables individual defendants to be convicted of, and sentenced for, an offence which properly represents their contribution to the overall fraud. We have explained how, without conspiracy to defraud, it might be difficult or impossible to secure a conviction for *any* offence against persons who play minor roles in the fraud, because they have insufficient knowledge of the details to be charged with aiding and abetting the

---

[6]   Criminal Law Revision Committee, Eighteenth Report: Conspiracy to Defraud (1986), Cmnd 9873.

[7]   eg *Tonner* [1985] 1 WLR 344; *Cox and Mead, The Times* 6 December 1984; *Lloyd* [1985] QB 829; *Grant* (1985) 82 Cr App R 324. See, in Appendix B below, the CLRC's Eighteenth Report: Conspiracy to Defraud (1986), Cmnd 9873, paras 3.3-3.10.

[8]   The CLRC referred to *Pain, Jory and Hawkins* [1985] Crim LR 215, a case of a conspiracy to defraud Chanel Ltd by selling bogus Chanel products: under the *Ayres* rule the prosecution was reduced to charging substantive offences under the Trade Descriptions Act 1968, which related to the minor frauds perpetrated on the purchasers rather than the major fraud on the company. See, in Appendix B below, the CLRC's Eighteenth Report: Conspiracy to Defraud (1986), Cmnd 9873, para 3.12.

substantive offences committed by those at the centre of the scheme.[9] To this extent conspiracy to defraud serves to fill a gap which might otherwise exist. But even if *some* offence can be proved against a person on the fringe of the scheme, it may be more appropriate that he should be convicted in respect of the overall fraud than in respect only of the offence which constitutes his own contribution thereto.

5.6   For example, the ringleader, A, might procure B to steal cheque forms from a bank, C to forge cheques and D to obtain money by passing them off as genuine. B and C cannot necessarily be charged with conspiracy to obtain money by deception, because they may not know the details of the intended deceptions; but they will know in general terms that they are participating in a fraud, and they can therefore be charged with conspiracy to defraud—which better represents the criminality of their conduct than the theft or the forgery alone. As one prosecutor put it, conspiracy to defraud reflects the criminality not only of the overall fraud, but also of everyone in it.

C.   SIMPLIFYING THE TRIAL

5.7   Even if the commission of substantive offences is central to the fraud, it does not follow that it is appropriate to charge those offences (or conspiracies to commit them) rather than conspiracy to defraud. In many cases such a course will fragment the allegations in such a way as to render the indictment unnecessarily long and confusing and the trial unnecessarily protracted.

5.8   There appear to be two main reasons for including an unmanageably large number of counts in an indictment for fraud. In the first place the fraud may have involved a large number of *transactions*: for example, funds may have been stolen by means of numerous transfers from a bank account over a substantial period. A single count alleging theft of the total would be bad for duplicity. The only way to reduce the indictment to reasonable proportions is to lay specimen counts in respect of some transactions only. However, this may render inadmissible the evidence relating to the rest.

5.9   There is also a danger that the sentence may fail to reflect the gravity of the overall fraud. Where the defendant has committed a large number of similar offences, it is common practice for the charges to be limited to a comparatively small number of "specimen counts" which are representative of the larger number of offences that the defendant is alleged to have committed.[10] If the defendant pleads guilty to the

---

[9]   See paras 4.69-4.72 above.

[10]   If, eg, the defendant has obtained a giro cheque by way of social security benefit every week for 3 years, a single count of obtaining 156 cheques by deception would be bad for duplicity.

specimen charges *on the basis that he has committed only the offences to which those charges relate*, he can be sentenced only for those offences.[11]

5.10 One possible solution to this problem, assuming that there is sufficient evidence of a conspiracy, is to charge one count of statutory conspiracy to commit numerous substantive offences. But it may be that the individual transactions are such as would require not just distinct counts but counts for different substantive *offences*, for example because they involve the obtaining by deception of different kinds of benefit—property, services, the execution of valuable securities and so on. It is impossible to charge a statutory conspiracy to commit a variety of different offences. In such a case the only way to reflect the overall fraud, while keeping the indictment manageable, is to charge conspiracy to defraud.

5.11 A typical social security fraud, for example, may involve instances of theft (of a benefit book), forgery, false accounting and obtaining by deception. Some of the defendants may be alleged to have been party to some of these offences but not others. If the indictment consists of four counts alleging conspiracies to steal, to forge, falsely to account and to obtain by deception, with each defendant appearing in some counts but not others, the jury is required to determine whether each defendant was party to the particular conspiracy or conspiracies alleged against him. The summing-up must deal with the evidence on that issue, for every defendant and every count. The result can be regrettably complicated. On a single count of conspiracy to defraud, on the other hand, the jury can simply be asked to consider whether each of the defendants has been proved to have been a party to the overall fraud. In the event of a conviction the judge can sentence according to his view of the part played by each defendant.

5.12 A second reason for the proliferation of counts within a fraud indictment is the structure of the existing law of dishonesty, particularly that relating to deception. Because of the way in which the individual offences are defined it may sometimes be impossible to contain even a single transaction within a single count. One example cited to us by the Serious Fraud Office involved the procuring by deception of the transfer of funds in the form of both cash and stock from two different pension funds: to charge substantive offences in respect of this one transaction would have required no fewer than four counts.

D. THE AVOIDANCE OF TECHNICALITIES

5.13 A further point, closely related to the last, is the difficulty of explaining some of the

---

[11] *McKenzie* (1984) 6 Cr App R (S) 99; *Burfoot* (1991) 12 Cr App R (S) 252; *Archbold* (1993 ed) para 5-35.

substantive offences of dishonesty to a jury. Concepts such as that of a thing in action,[12] or a valuable security,[13] are not easy to grasp. There is of course a certain threshold of legal understanding that the jury must be asked to attain in any trial; but it is in the interests of justice to keep that threshold as low as possible.

> The law of theft is in urgent need of simplification so that a jury of twelve citizens does not have to grapple with concepts couched in the antiquated "franglais" of "choses in action" and scarce public resources of time and money are not devoted to hours of semantic arguments divorced from the true merits of the case.[14]

E.   SENTENCE

5.14   Conspiracy to defraud is punishable with up to ten years' imprisonment, even where it is essentially no more than a conspiracy to commit a comparatively minor substantive offence and, if charged as that offence or as a statutory conspiracy to commit it,[15] would attract a much lighter maximum sentence. As we explained above,[16] this fact can in principle be regarded as a criticism of the offence; but, on the other hand, if the maximum sentence for the substantive offence (or the statutory conspiracy) is inadequate to reflect the gravity of the defendants' conduct, conspiracy to defraud gives the court the sentencing powers it needs.

5.15   An example referred to by the CLRC[17] is *Pain, Jory and Hawkins*,[18] where the defendants had conspired to manufacture and sell products falsely purporting to be made by Chanel Ltd. They were convicted of offences under section 1(1)(b) of the Trade Descriptions Act 1968, which carries a maximum of only two years' imprisonment.[19] Counts of conspiracy to defraud were held to be bad, because under the rule in *Ayres*[20] an agreement which amounted to a conspiracy to commit a substantive offence could not be charged as a conspiracy to defraud at common law; now that *Ayres* has been reversed by statute, convictions of conspiracy to defraud would enable realistic sentences to be imposed.

---

[12]   Theft Act 1968, s 4(1).

[13]   Theft Act 1968, s 20(2). Prosecutors are notoriously reluctant to use this offence even in those cases for which it is designed.

[14]   *Per* Beldam LJ in *Hallam, The Times* 27 May 1994, cited more fully at para 1.16, n 35 above.

[15]   Criminal Law Act 1977, s 3.

[16]   See paras 3.14-3.16.

[17]   Criminal Law Revision Committee, Eighteenth Report: Conspiracy to Defraud (1986) Cmnd 9873, para 3.12; see Appendix B below.

[18]   [1985] Crim LR 215.

[19]   The convictions were quashed because the charges had been laid out of time.

[20]   [1984] AC 447; para 1.8 above.

F. SUMMARY

5.16 In our view the practical considerations discussed above represent compelling reasons for retaining the offence of conspiracy to defraud at least for the time being, as a means of simplifying and shortening fraud trials and enabling individual defendants to be convicted of an offence appropriate to their conduct. We do not rule out the possibility of eventually reconciling concern for these considerations with some narrowing of the law, for example by means of changes in the law relating to indictments and procedure. But we cannot recommend any further restriction on prosecutors' use of the offence unless and until ways can be found of preserving its practical advantages for the administration of justice.

(Signed) HENRY BROOKE, *Chairman*
ANDREW BURROWS
DIANA FABER
CHARLES HARPUM
STEPHEN SILBER

MICHAEL SAYERS, *Secretary*
11 October 1994

APPENDIX A

Draft
Theft (Amendment) Bill

ARRANGEMENT OF CLAUSES

DRAFT

OF A

B I L L

INTITULED

An Act to make provision with respect to the dishonest obtaining of loans.

A.D. 1994.

B E IT ENACTED by the Queen's most Excellent Majesty, by and with the advice and consent of the Lords Spiritual and Temporal, and Commons, in this present Parliament assembled, and by the authority of the same, as follows:—

5   **1.** In section 1 of the Theft Act 1978 (offence of obtaining services by deception), after subsection (2) (circumstances where there is an obtaining of services) there shall be added—

> "(3) Without prejudice to the generality of subsection (2) above, it
> 10   is an obtaining of services where the other is induced to make a
> loan, or to cause or permit a loan to be made, on the understanding
> that any payment (whether by way of interest or otherwise) will be
> or has been made in respect of the loan."

Offence of obtaining services by deception extends to loans.

1978 c. 31.

  2.—(1) This Act may be cited as the Theft (Amendment) Act 1994.

  (2) This Act shall come into force at the end of the period of two
15 months beginning with the day on which this Act is passed.

  (3) Section 1 does not have effect in relation to anything done before the coming into force of this Act.

  (4) This Act extends to England and Wales only.

Short title, commencement and extent.

EXPLANATORY NOTES

Clause 1 implements a recommendation which is dealt with in paragraphs 4.30-4.33. It amends section 1 of the Theft Act 1978 so as to make clear that the offence under that section of dishonestly obtaining services by deception includes dishonestly inducing a person by deception to make a loan, or to cause or permit a loan to be made, on the understanding that any payment, whether by way of interest or otherwise, will be or has been made in respect of the loan.

Clause 2 provides for the short title and commencement date, that the amendment made by Clause 1 does not have any effect in relation to anything done before the coming into force of the Act, and that the Act extends to England and Wales only.

APPENDIX B

Extract from the Eighteenth Report of the Criminal Law Revision Committee, Conspiracy to Defraud (1986), Cmnd 9873

PART III. THE LAW SINCE AYRES

Introduction

3.1   A number of decisions of the Court of Appeal have shown that contrary to expectation the *Ayres* decision has on occasion led to justice not being done. The Court of Appeal has had to quash convictions where there were no merits, permitting large-scale frauds to go unpunished or inadequately punished. As one judge commented to us, these appeals are not brought on the basis that a charge of conspiracy to defraud was unfair or produced a wrong verdict, but on technical grounds aimed at evading conviction or achieving a lesser sentence. We agree.

3.2   The following cases illustrate how rogues can escape punishment, or adequate punishment, which must be a matter of public concern. Apart altogether from this, it will be seen that *Ayres* causes difficulty for trial judges, prosecutors and juries.

R v Tonner[1]

3.3   One class of case where *Ayres* has caused difficulty has been where the commission of a substantive offence is merely incidental to a larger fraud which has been perpetrated. In *Tonner* the appellants were charged with conspiracy to defraud contrary to common law. There were alternative counts of statutory conspiracy contrary to section 1(1) of the Criminal Law Act 1977, the particulars of which specified contravention of section 38(1) of the Finance Act 1972 and section 170(2) of the Customs and Excise Management Act 1979. The charge of conspiring to defraud was chosen for two reasons: to enable a complicated set of transactions involving a number of possible offences to be presented to the jury more simply, and to ensure that the fraud was adequately punished, the penalty being at large. Tonner and his co-defendants had obtained gold without paying value added tax on it (some was smuggled in, some was in the form of gold currency, on the purchase of which value added tax was not at that time payable). The gold was melted down and sold to bullion dealers, who were charged the tax on the sale. The tax was not, however, paid over to Customs and Excise. The amount of tax involved was some £3 million. The appellants were convicted on the counts alleging conspiracy to defraud; Tonner received a total of 7½ years' imprisonment and was fined £400,000, and his co-defendants received 4½ and 2 years' imprisonment respectively.[2] No verdicts were taken on the counts alleging the statutory conspiracies, which were ordered to lie on the file.

3.4   Expressing regret, the Court of Appeal quashed the convictions, ruling that after *Ayres* the course taken by the Crown was no longer open to prosecutors. In *Tonner* the Court was able to substitute convictions on some of the charges left on the file.[3] But the

---

[1]   [1985] 1 WLR 344.

[2]   Suspended sentences were activated in the case of Tonner and one of his co-defendants.

[3]   By reason of section 3(1) of the Criminal Appeal Act 1968 which provides for this where the appellant has been convicted of an offence and it appears to the Court of Appeal that on the finding of the jury they must have been satisfied of facts which proved him guilty of

maximum punishment for conviction on those offences was then 2 years' imprisonment[4] and a penalty of three times the tax withheld from the Revenue. The Court, being precluded by *Ayres* from upholding the sentences which the trial judge had awarded, tried to mark the seriousness of the offence by awarding Tonner the maximum 2 years on each of the two counts on which convictions were substituted, to run consecutively, together with fines totalling £400,000. The other defendants each received 2 years' imprisonment.

3.5 *R v Cox and Mead*.[5] This was a case of long firm fraud, that is, buying goods on credit, selling them below cost and not paying for them as a sustained course of defrauding the suppliers. C was convicted of conspiracy to defraud; M was acquitted of conspiracy to defraud but was convicted of fraudulent trading. On appeal, it was held, applying *Ayres* and *Tonner*, that the conspiracy to defraud count was bad because the conspiracy involved the commission of a number of substantive offences. (The Court of Appeal was unable to apply the proviso to section 2 of the Criminal Appeal Act 1968 because of the way the indictment had been drafted.) However, the Court of Appeal substituted a verdict of guilty on a count charging conspiracy to obtain property and services by deception. Counsel for the Crown said, as he is recorded in the judgment, that the construction put upon the 1977 Act caused difficulties for prosecutors:

> before a count of conspiracy to defraud can be put into an indictment, the case has to be examined in detail both for the purpose of seeing whether the evidence involves any substantive offence, such as a minor one under the Companies Act 1948 and whether in the course of cross-examination of the prosecution's witnesses such an offence may be disclosed.

This illustrated the difficulties which prosecutors have, and our Chairman [Lawton LJ], who was a member of the Court of Appeal in this case, drew attention to the fact that before 1977 it had been the practice to indict in long firm fraud cases for conspiracy to defraud. "Explaining the charge to the jury was easy. They would be asked to decide whether the victims had been swindled and, if they had been, whether each of the defendants had been proved to have been a party to the swindle." However, that course was no longer open to the prosecution.

3.6 *R v Lloyd*[6] was another case of this kind. Feature films were clandestinely removed by Lloyd from the cinema where he worked and then copied and returned. The pirated copies were then sold. This kind of conduct caused substantial loss to the owners of the copyright in the films. The appellants were convicted of conspiracy to steal, and an alternative count of conspiracy to defraud was ordered to lie on the file. The Court of Appeal quashed the convictions, holding that the borrowing and copying did not in law amount to theft (notwithstanding the serious loss likely to be suffered by the owners of the films). The Court declined to reactivate the charge of conspiracy to defraud, since it was conceded that the agreement among the appellants amounted to a conspiracy to contravene section 1 of the Copyright Act 1956. The penalties under that section were minimal; they have since been increased,[7] but they are still hardly

---

another offence.

[4] Since increased to 7 years.

[5] *The Times*, 6 December 1984.

[6] [1985] QB 829.

[7] By the Copyright (Amendment) Act 1983, s 1(3). The maximum penalty is now 2 years' imprisonment.

adequate for such a case extending over a long period and involving numerous and profitable acts of piracy. Before the 1977 Act the defendants could have been charged with common law conspiracy to defraud and if convicted punished appropriately.[8]

3.7   *R v Grant*.[9] The difficulties created by *Ayres* were apparent to the Court of Appeal in *Grant*. The appellant was convicted at the end of a 3 month trial of conspiracy to defraud and sentenced to 3½ years' imprisonment. With another man, who was facing proceedings abroad, the appellant had operated a scheme under which private individuals were invited to subscribe money with a view to purchasing an interest in holiday chalets which were to be erected in the Canary Islands. In its inception the scheme was honest, although it was risky and the brochures were over-optimistic. As the scheme ran into difficulties, however, the promoters began to engage in deception. When the appellant was arrested in 1982, more than 200 people had paid money into the scheme. Their losses came to some £650,000, most of which had gone to benefit the appellant and his partner.

3.8   The decision of the House of Lords in *Ayres* was not yet available when the indictment was framed, but the difficulty in laying a single charge of conspiracy to defraud embracing the scheme as an entirety was appreciated after the decision in *Duncalf*.[10] Counsel nevertheless chose that course in the interest of simplifying the issues. "He appreciated that simplicity was likely to result in justice to both sides, complication in justice to neither." The particulars of the offence in the indictment were given as conspiracy to defraud investors by dishonestly making false or reckless statements to prospective or actual investors; failing to disclose the absence of planning consent for the chalets; and fraudulently obtaining the release of investors' funds held in a special joint account. During the trial Counsel for the appellant submitted that those particulars disclosed a conspiracy or conspiracies to commit specific statutory offences and that the indictment alleging conspiracy to defraud was therefore defective. The Judge did not accept the submission and left the matter to the jury as follows: Had it been proved that there was an agreement to which the appellant was a party, to induce others to act to their detriment by exposing those others to the risks of possible injury which they would not have run in the absence of the deceit?

3.9   In the course of the appeal, counsel for the appellant drew up a "ghost indictment", containing 10 counts of conspiracy to commit substantive offences of dishonesty. The Court of Appeal reluctantly concluded that the conspiracy was indeed one to contravene one or more provisions of the Theft Act 1968 and that the Crown was not able to allege a common law conspiracy to defraud. The Court said that since *Ayres* trials had become longer and more complex and the issues more difficult for juries to understand. The "ghost indictment" illustrated this.

3.10   However, the Court was able to apply the proviso to section 2(1) of the Criminal Appeal Act 1968, on the ground that once the jury concluded that the appellant had acted dishonestly, "the rest of the ingredients of the offence of conspiracy to obtain property by deception inevitably fell into place." The misdescription of the appellants' conduct led to no injustice; the appeal was accordingly dismissed.[11]

---

[8]   See *Scott v Metropolitan Police Commr.* ... .

[9]   *The Times*, 24 December 1985.

[10]   (1979) 69 Cr App R 206 (conspiracy to steal by shoplifting), approved by the House of Lords in *Ayres*.

[11]   As in *Ayres* itself.

3.11　The second kind of case in which *Ayres* has caused difficulties is when in the course of carrying out a fraud on the victim the defendant commits an offence against a third party, which may be a minor one. Since *Ayres* the victim is unprotected by the law, as the next case we mention illustrates.

3.12　*Pain, Jory and Hawkins*.[12] In *Pain, Jory and Hawkins* the original indictment charged the appellants with conspiracy to defraud Chanel Limited by the manufacture and sale of bogus Chanel products. At the trial it was successfully submitted that these counts were bad since the carrying out of the conspiracy involved substantive offences against the Trade Descriptions Act 1968. New counts of offences against the 1968 Act were substituted and the defendants were convicted. On appeal it was successfully argued that the new charges had been preferred out of time. The convictions were therefore quashed. After *Pain, Jory and Hawkins,* therefore, this kind of serious counterfeiting cannot be charged as a conspiracy to defraud. The penalties under the Trade Descriptions Act 1968 (which is for the protection of buyers) are not adequate, and were not intended to deal with large scale frauds.[13]

Further difficulties

3.15　... it may be difficult at the outset or even in the course of the trial to discern whether any substantive offence (including a statutory conspiracy) is involved. When evidence of such an offence, which as we have shown may be a minor one, does emerge, then the judge has to direct the jury not to return a verdict on the charge of conspiracy to defraud. Instead they will be told to give their attention solely to the evidence relating to the added substantive offence. This may confuse the jury.

3.16　Moreover, the addition of further counts to the indictment may not always be possible. It is only possible where the offences are the subject of committal charges (which *ex hypothesi* is ruled out in the sort of case where the evidence only emerges at a later stage) or where the new charges can be founded on the committal documents.[14] There is an element of chance here. Unless these conditions apply, the trial must be abandoned and new proceedings instituted. It is necessary too for the trial judge to take care before allowing the indictment to be amended that the accused is not taken by surprise and thereby prejudiced by the new course the trial will take.

3.17　There is too a possible difficulty in sentencing where the Crown is precluded from charging conspiracy to defraud by reason of the existence of an incidental substantive offence. If in such a case the defendant pleads not guilty to common law conspiracy (as he will since *Ayres*) and guilty to the minor substantive offence, the following problems arise. As has been shown, the substantive offence or offences to which he pleads guilty may not reflect the true essence of the fraud. Secondly, the judge may be precluded from considering the loss suffered by the intended victim. If the case had been presented on the basis that the substantive charges were merely samples of the whole, then the extent of the loss would probably be investigated, but not otherwise. A plea of guilty might be tendered on the basis that the substantive offence stood on its own and represented the sole extent of the defendant's involvement, whereas the Crown would probably contend that his involvement was more extensive. This issue on a plea of guilty might cause difficulty for the judge, since it might turn out to

---

[12]　[1985] Crim LR 215.

[13]　The maximum penalty for contravening section 1(1)(b) of the 1968 Act is two years' imprisonment: s 18. By making two of Jory's sentences run consecutively, the trial judge was able to award him 3 years; the other defendants received respectively 18 months' and 4 months' imprisonment (suspended).

[14]　Administration of Justice (Miscellaneous Provisions) Act 1933, s 2(2), proviso (i).

require a trial of some substance in which a jury would play no part.[15]

3.18   For all these reasons, we are sure that the law ought not to be left in its present state.

---

[15] *Newton* (1983) 77 Cr App R 187.

APPENDIX C

Fraud Offences Tried in the Crown Court:England & Wales 1982-92[1]

Obtaining property by deception (Theft Act 1968, s.15)

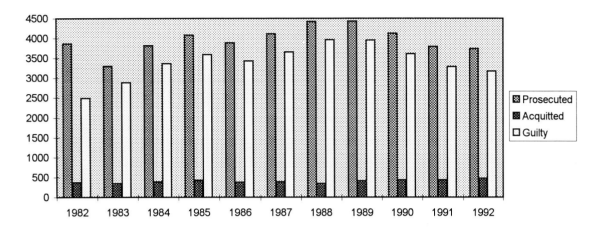

Conspiracy to defraud

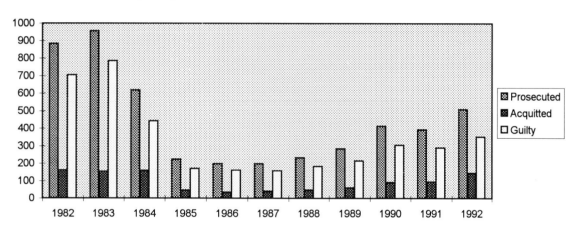

All other offences of fraud[2]

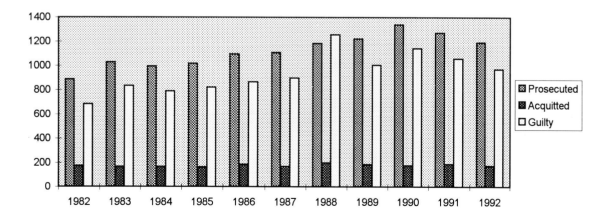

[1] The statistics quoted were supplied to us by the Home Office.

[2] Viz. False statements by company directors; Fraudulently inducing persons to invest money; Other frauds by company directors; False accounting; Obtaining pecuniary advantage by deception; Dishonestly procuring execution of a document; Obtaining services by deception; Evasion of liability by deception; Making off without payment; Other frauds.

APPENDIX D

Statutory Provisions Relating to Offences of Fraud, Deception and Computer Misuse

Gaming Act 1845, s 17

17 Every person who shall, by any fraud or unlawful device or ill practice in playing at or with cards, dice, tables, or other game, or in bearing a part in the stakes, wagers, or adventures, or in betting on the sides or hands of them that do play, or in wagering on the event of any game, sport, pastime, or exercise, win from any other person to himself, or any other or others, any sum of money or valuable thing, shall

    (a)   on conviction on indictment be liable to imprisonment for a term not exceeding two years;

    (b)   on summary conviction be liable to imprisonment for a term not exceeding six months or to a fine not exceeding the prescribed sum [currently £5,000].

Theft Act 1968, ss 15, 16 and 20(2)

15 (1) A person who by any deception dishonestly obtains property belonging to another, with the intention of permanently depriving the other of it, shall on conviction on indictment be liable to imprisonment for a term not exceeding ten years.

(2) For purposes of this section a person is to be treated as obtaining property if he obtains ownership, possession or control of it, and "obtain" includes obtaining for another or enabling another to obtain or to retain.

(3) Section 6 above [which relates to the requisite intention in theft of permanently depriving the owner of property] shall apply for purposes of this section, with the necessary adaptation of the reference to appropriating, as it applies for purposes of section 1.

(4) For purposes of this section "deception" means any deception (whether deliberate or reckless) by words or conduct as to fact or as to law, including a deception as to the present intentions of the person using the deception or any other person.

16 (1) A person who by any deception dishonestly obtains for himself or another any pecuniary advantage shall on conviction on indictment be liable to imprisonment for a term not exceeding five years.

(2) The cases in which a pecuniary advantage within the meaning of this section is to be regarded as obtained for a person are cases where—

    (a)   [repealed]

    (b)   he is allowed to borrow by way of overdraft, or to take out any policy of insurance or annuity contract, or obtains an improvement of the terms on which he is allowed to do so; or

    (c)   he is given the opportunity to earn remuneration or greater remuneration in an office or employment, or to win money by betting.

(3) For purposes of this section "deception" has the same meaning as in section 15 of this Act.

20 (2) A person who dishonestly, with a view to gain for himself or another or with intent to cause loss to another, by any deception procures the execution of a valuable security shall on conviction on indictment be liable to imprisonment for a term not exceeding seven years; and this subsection shall apply in relation to the making, acceptance, indorsement, alteration, cancellation or destruction in whole or in part of a valuable security, and in relation to the signing or sealing of any paper or other material in order that it may be made or converted into, or used or dealt with as, a valuable security, as if that were the execution of a valuable security.

Theft Act 1978, ss 1-5
1 (1) A person who by any deception dishonestly obtains services from another shall be guilty of an offence.

(2) It is an obtaining of services where the other is induced to confer a benefit by doing some act, or causing or permitting some act to be done, on the understanding that the benefit has been or will be paid for.

2 (1) Subject to subsection (2) below, where a person by any deception—

    (a)   dishonestly secures the remission of the whole or part of any existing liability to make a payment, whether his own liability or another's; or

    (b)   with intent to make permanent default in whole or in part on any existing liability to make a payment, or with intent to let another do so, dishonestly induces the creditor or any person claiming payment on behalf of the creditor to wait for payment (whether or not the due date for payment is deferred) or to forgo payment; or

    (c)   dishonestly obtains any exemption from or abatement of liability to make a payment;

he shall be guilty of an offence.

(2) For purposes of this section "liability" means legally enforceable liability; and subsection (1) shall not apply in relation to a liability that has not been accepted or established to pay compensation for a wrongful act or omission.

(3) For purposes of subsection (1)(b) a person induced to take in payment a cheque or other security for money by way of conditional satisfaction of a pre-existing liability is to be treated not as being paid but as being induced to wait for payment.

(4) For purposes of subsection (1)(c) "obtains" includes obtaining for another or enabling another to obtain.

3 (1) Subject to subsection (3) below, a person who, knowing that payment on the spot for any goods supplied or service done is required or expected from him, dishonestly makes off without having paid as required or expected and with intent to avoid payment of the amount due shall be guilty of an offence.

(2) For purposes of this section "payment on the spot" includes payment at the time of collecting goods on which work has been done or in respect of which service has been provided.

(3) Subsection (1) above shall not apply where the supply of the goods or the doing of the service is contrary to law, or where the service done is such that payment is not legally enforceable.

(4) Any person may arrest without warrant anyone who is, or whom he, with reasonable cause, suspects to be, committing or attempting to commit an offence under this section.

4 (1) Offences under this Act shall be punishable either on conviction on indictment or on summary conviction.

(2) A person convicted on indictment shall be liable—

    (a)   for an offence under section 1 or section 2 of this Act, to imprisonment for a term not exceeding five years; and

    (b)   for an offence under section 3 of this Act, to imprisonment for a term not exceeding two years.

(3) A person convicted summarily of any offence under this Act shall be liable—

    (a)   to imprisonment for a term not exceeding six months; or

    (b)   to a fine not exceeding the prescribed sum for the purposes of [section 32 of the Magistrates' Courts Act 1980] (punishment on summary conviction of offences triable either way ...) [currently £5,000],

or to both.

5 (1) For purposes of sections 1 and 2 above "deception" has the same meaning as in section 15 of the Theft Act 1968 ... .

Computer Misuse Act 1990, s 1
1 (1) A person is guilty of an offence if—

    (a)   he causes a computer to perform any function with intent to secure access to any program or data held in any computer;

    (b)   the access he intends to secure is unauthorised; and

    (c)   he knows at the time when he causes the computer to perform the function that that is the case.

(2) The intent a person has to have to commit an offence under this section need not be directed at—

    (a)   any particular program or data;

    (b)   a program or data of any particular kind; or

    (c)   a program or data held in any particular computer.

(3) A person guilty of an offence under this section shall be liable on summary conviction to imprisonment for a term not exceeding six months or to a fine not exceeding level 5 on the standard scale [currently £5,000] or to both.

APPENDIX E

List of persons and organisations who commented on Working Paper No 104

Association of Chief Police Officers of England, Wales and Northern Ireland
Lord Benson GBE
British Telecom
Mr David Butler
Professor Richard Card
Confederation of British Industry
Judge Michael Coombe
The Council of Her Majesty's Circuit Judges
Criminal Bar Association
Crown Prosecution Service
Department of Trade and Industry
Department of Trade and Industry, Insolvency Service
Mr David Fitzpatrick
Miss Isabel Gurney
Dr A H Hermann [article in the *Financial Times*, 28 February 1988]
Home Office
Inland Revenue [Crime Section]
The Institute of Chartered Accountants in England and Wales
The Institute of Legal Executives
Justice
The Justices' Clerks' Society
The Law Society
The Law Society, Young Solicitors' Group
Sir Frederick Lawton
Lord Chancellor's Department
Metropolitan and City Police Company Fraud Department
National Computing Centre
Mr Justice Phillips
The Police Superintendents' Association of England and Wales
Judge James Rant QC
Lord Roskill
Serious Fraud Office
Securities and Investment Board
Professor A T H Smith [article: [1988] Crim LR 508]
Society of Public Teachers of Law
Mr G R Sullivan [articles: [1988] Crim LJ 288; [1989] Crim LJ 92]
Lord Justice Woolf

Printed in the United Kingdom for HMSO
Dd 5063291 · 12/94 · c14 · 39462 · 3398/8B · 306762